Missions Moments

Mitzi Eaker

Woman's Missionary Union®
Birmingham, Alabama

Woman's Missionary Union, SBC
P. O. Box 830010
Birmingham, AL 35283-0010

For more information, visit our Web site at www.wmu.com or
call 1-800-968-7301.

Dewey Decimal Classification: 226.07
Subject Heading: MISSION ACTION
                 MINISTRY
                 RELIGIOUS EDUCATION—YOUTH

Cover design by Bruce Watford
Design by Janell E. Young

ISBN: 1-56309-943-8
ISBN: 978-1-56309-943-4
W057113•1205•1M2

Shane Eaker, you are a blessing. I could not have written this without your continual love, support, encouragement, and prayers. You are a wonderful helpmate.

This book is a gift to Micah, Joshua, Lydia, Caleb, and future generations of Gibbses and Eakers.

Contents

Acknowledgements

I could not have completed this book without the support of my husband, Shane; my best friend, Denise Roebuck; and my parents, Martha and Larry Gibbs. They were determined that I could do it. Also, Lorie Mattox and Barbara Joiner continually supported me through the process. Of course, I could not do it without complete reliance on God.

I want to thank those who laid a foundation of faith and missions in my life: Larry and Martha Gibbs, the Girls in Action® organization, Richard Bradford, Bob Ford, Gary Britton, and Renee Schuler Wilson. Thanks to those who taught me about Christian education and leadership: Carey Newman, Jim Cobban, Stanley Togikawa, Walter Thweatt, Jerry Rea, James Blakeney, and Joye Smith. Thanks to my prayer warriors: Beverly, Ashley, Traci, Amy, Katie, Gary, Gayle, Esther, and Joan. Special thanks to the many friends and family members who supported me through the process.

And I cannot thank enough those organizations that have invested in my life: Cherokee Baptist Association, Baptist Campus Ministries, Alabama Baptist Convention, Hawaii Pacific Baptist Convention, Alabama WMU, Etowah Baptist Association, WMU, and the Women on Mission® group of Slackland Baptist Church.

Special thanks to Nancy Fritz, Karen Hardin, and Jill Harris of the Caleb Project. It was through encountering their passion for children's missions education that this book was conceived. And to my colleagues who supported me through the project: Scott Goggins, Delores Jackson, Amy Bailey, and Children's Resource Team of WMU.

Introduction

During one of my trips as the children's consultant for national Woman's Missionary Union® (WMU®), I attended a missions conference sponsored by the Caleb Project. In one of the small-group breakout sessions, several children's ministers and church leaders discussed the need for more children's missions education. We shared how a generation is taught basic spiritual disciplines, but they are taught little about seeing people beyond themselves and how to minister to them. As we talked, the concept for the book was formed. The book should include a missions education message to be used in children's sermons, an activity to stress the message, and an activity challenging parents and their children to become involved in missions. At the end of the discussion, one of the Caleb Project representatives asked when I was going to write this book. Fortunately, WMU® liked the concept and I began the writing process.

Missions Moments is designed to encourage pastors, children's workers, and parents to teach children the foundation of the Christian faith and missions. This book is not designed to replace ongoing church-based missons education, but as a supplemental piece to church programs that do not have a missions element. The chapters are designed for three different settings. The first setting is a 3- to 5-minute children's message during the worship service. The Message highlights an area of missions for the pastor or children's minister to teach children. The second setting is a 15-minute supplemental piece in a classroom. The children's worker presents the Message and leads the children in the Application Activity. The third setting is a 20-minute family devotion time. The parent presents the Message, leads the children in the Application Activity, and closes with the Family Moment. After completing all 52 chapters, there are family debriefing questions to reflect on what the family has learned about missions or how they have become involved in missions.

Working through the 52 chapters will provide a foundation for children to understand the joy of being on mission with God. The chapters cover the foundations of the Christian faith, the foundations of a missions lifestyle, how missionaries serve, and potential ministry opportunities. "Foundations of Faith" teaches where to find the truth about God and the basic principles of faith and salvation. "Foundations of Missional Living" teaches about living for God. "Foundations of Missions" shows what it is like to be a missionary and gives examples of how people are to serve God. "Ministry" focuses on ministries that are reaching people for Christ.

1.

Foundations
of Faith

1. Who Is God?

Scripture Passage: Luke 1:1–4

Verse to Memorize: Luke 1:4

Missional Lesson: The truth about God is in the Bible.

Message

Materials Needed: A poster with *God* written on one side and *Bible* written on the other

I want to ask you the most often asked question in the whole wide world. The question is, Who is God? (*Hold up the sign with the word* God.) What is your answer?

People everywhere have different answers to this question. As Christians, we believe there is only one place to find the answer to this question. Do you know where we find the answer to Who is God?

(*Hold up the sign with the word* Bible.) The Bible is correct. The Bible is a special book about God. It is special because God told many people what to write.

Here are just a few things that the Bible says about God. In Genesis, the first book of the Bible, we learn that God created the world and everything in it, including you and me. In the Old Testament we learn that God keeps His promises. In the New Testament we learn that God sent His Son, Jesus, to teach us about God. And in the whole Bible we see how God loves the people of the world. In the Bible, we also learn about how God has a purpose for each of us.

I want to encourage each of you to get a Bible you can understand and read it every day or have someone read it to you so that you can learn more about God. Let's end in prayer.

Prayer: God, thank You for creating the world. Thank You for writing the Bible so that we may learn about You.

Application Activity: Scripture Interpretations

Materials Needed: Bibles, paper, and pencils or crayons
Challenge to the Children: Read the Bible every day this week to learn Who God is.

For children who can read, prepare a piece of paper with the question *What do the following verses teach me about God?* at the top and a list of verses with enough space for the children to write their answers (see following verses). During the activity, give every child a Bible, a piece of paper with the question and verses, and a pencil. Have the readers read each verse, answer the question, and move to the next verse. Assist younger children in finding the verses. After about seven minutes, go over the answers with the children.

For children who cannot read, give every child a blank piece of paper and crayons. Have an adult read a verse (see following verses). Ask the children to draw what they learned and explain unfamiliar concepts about God from this verse. Give the children a moment to draw. Then ask the children to say what they learned about God from the verse. Read another verse and repeat the process.

Verses:

Genesis 1:1 (Creator)
Leviticus 19:2 (Holy)
Leviticus 26:12 (Personal)
Deuteronomy 7:9 (Faithful)
John 10:10 (Life Giver)
Jeremiah 29:11 (Purpose)
Romans 5:8 (Jesus)

Family Moment

Share a story from your life when the Bible helped you know Who God is.

2. God Loves Me

Scripture Passages: John 3:16; Romans 5:8

Verse to Memorize: Romans 5:8

Missional Lesson: Children will learn of God's plan of salvation.

Message

Materials Needed: Pictures that represent Jesus' life, death, and resurrection

Let's read John 3:16. (*Read John 3:16.*) This verse says God loved the world so much that He sent Jesus to the earth. Jesus came to earth and showed us how to live. Jesus taught us about God's love for you and me.

The Bible says that everyone has sin in his or her life, and sin separates us from God. Sin came into the world through Adam and Eve choosing to disobey God. However, God had a plan to send Jesus to earth. When Jesus came to earth, He didn't sin. He is the only human who did not sin. (*Show the pictures of Jesus' life, death, and resurrection.*) And when Jesus died, He took our sins way. But He came back to life three days later. Jesus lived, died, and came back to life because He wanted to make a way for us to not be separated from God by our sins. God did this because He loves us. How can we show God we understand His love for us?

First, you must hear and learn about Jesus.

Second, you must confess your sins to God and ask for His forgiveness.

Third, you must believe that Jesus is God's Son, He lived a life without sin, and that He died and came back to life. You must believe that God loves you so much that He asked Jesus to do this for you.

Then you will want to commit your life to following Jesus. And that is how we show God we understand His love for us. Let us pray.

Prayer: God, help us to learn about Jesus and how much You love us.

Application Activity: Matching Game

Materials Needed: Fourteen craft sticks and an empty coffee can

Challenge: Read John 3:16 every day this week, and remember God loves you.

Print each of the following Bible reference on two different craft sticks: Romans 5:8; Romans 6:23; Romans 3:23; 1 John 1:9; Acts 16:31; Romans 10:9; John 14:15. Place the sticks in an empty coffee can or something comparable so that none of the print is showing.

Invite each child to play a matching game using Bible verses about becoming a Christian. Call for one child to choose 2 craft sticks from the can. If the sticks have the same Bible reference on them, find the verse in the Bible and read it aloud. The child may keep the sticks and take another turn. If the verses do not match, he or she returns the sticks to the can without any part of the verse showing. Another child takes a turn choosing 2 sticks. Continue play until all the sticks have been matched.

. Let children locate and read one of the verses from a craft stick. Tell the children that God loves each one of us. Give each child a copy of the verses to take home.

Family Moment

If you are a Christian, share with your children about how you learned that God loved you. If you are not a Christian, please read the verses and pray about how these verses relate to you and your family.

3. God Loves the World

Scripture Passage: John 3:16

Verse to Memorize: John 3:16

Missional Lesson: God loves the world.

Message

Materials Needed: Five or six pictures of people of different ethnic and socioeconomic levels

(*Open by reading John 3:16.*) Last week we talked about how God loves you. Today I want to talk about God's love for all the people of the world. God created everything in the world and He said His creation was good. However, God gave each person a choice to obey Him or to disobey Him. The first humans, Adam and Eve, chose to disobey God.

When they disobeyed God, it separated them from God. When Adam disobeyed God, he sinned. At that point, sin entered the world God had created and separated every person from God.

Don't worry, God had a plan. God sent Jesus to the world to make a way for people to no longer be separated from God. The plan included the whole world. The Bible says that God wants all people to come back to Him. He provided a way for all the people in the world to come back to Him through Jesus.

I want to show you pictures of some of the people of the world, and I want you to tell me if God loves them and sent Jesus for them. (*Show five to six different pictures and let the children respond to each. Follow up after each picture by saying,* Yes, God loves them and sent Jesus for all people.)

God loves all people—those people like us, and those people who are different from us in every part of the world. He loved these people and He loved you so much that He sent Jesus to make a way for us to be with God. Let's pray.

Prayer: God, thank You for loving all the people of the world. Help me to love others as You do.

Application Activity: Picture Talk

Materials Needed: Use the pictures from the message above.

Challenge: When you see someone who looks, dresses, or acts different, remember God loves that person, too.

Show the pictures to the children again. After each picture, have the children talk about how it might be hard to talk to the person in the picture. Ask them questions such as What language would you need to learn? and How would you befriend this person? Have them think about how they could tell the person in the picture God loves them.

Ask them to share about people in their community who look and act different from them. Guide them to talk about ways that they can show God's love to those people. If time permits, have children role-play.

Family Moment

Discuss the people from different cultures and backgrounds you come in contact with throughout the week. Discuss how God loves all the people of the world.

4. Fearfully and Wonderfully Made

Scripture Passages: Genesis 1:27; Psalm 139:13–16

Verse to Memorize: Psalm 139:13

Missional Lesson: Children will learn that God is their creator and giver of life.

Message

(Have a mother bring her young baby and sit beside you. Introduce the mother and baby to the children.) Little *(baby's name)* is just *(number)* days old. Look how precious and delicate she is. Look at her tiny hands and feet.

At one time in our lives, we were all little babies. Do you know that God talks about babies in the Bible? He says in Psalm 139 that God made each of us while we were in our mother's womb. He says that we are perfectly and wonderfully made. In Genesis, God says that He made each of us in His image. God made you and gave you life. He created every part of you from the shape of your nose to the size of your toes. He made every part of you especially the way He wanted it.

Look at this baby's fingers. Now look at your fingers. Now look at my fingers. Even God planned how our fingers would grow. Isn't it amazing to see how God created us and to know that He gave us life? Let's thank God for making us.

Prayer: Thank You, God, for making us and giving us life.

Application Activity: Life-Size Portrait

Materials Needed: Butcher paper (large paper on a roll) or several sheets of white 8½-by-11 paper and markers
Challenge: Take the poster home and hang it on the wall. Each day write on the poster one or more things that you are grateful that God created about you.

Have each child make a life-size mural of himself or herself by using butcher paper. Cut butcher paper long enough for children to lie down on. Have an adult help outline each child on the paper. Then have the children draw how they see themselves. When they are finished, have them each write on their self-portrait, *I'm perfectly and wonderfully made by God.* If you do not have room to do a full-size portrait, have the children draw themselves on an 8½-by-11 sheet of paper.

Discuss how we can use the body that God created to honor Him. Encourage children to take their portrait home and hang it in their bedroom. Challenge them to write more things that they are grateful for that God created about them.

Family Moment

Share with your child the joy and excitement of that child's birth or adoption. Show your child pictures of himself or herself as a baby. Tell the child how special he or she is to you as well as to God.

5. Bible—God's Word

Scripture Passage: 2 Timothy 3:15–17

Verse to Memorize: James 1:22

Missional Lesson: Children will learn that the Bible teaches us about God and guides our lives.

Message

Materials Needed: A road map

(*Hold up a road map.*) Have you ever wished that you had a map for your life that would tell you where you were going next and guide you on what to do? Well, we do have a map that God gave us and it is called the Bible. In the Bible, we see the Big Picture. We see what God has been doing and He tells us His future plans. He even guides each of us on how to live.

God loved us so much that He provided the Bible as a guide for us to learn from and also obey. In 2 Timothy 3:16–17, the Bible says, "God has breathed life into all of Scripture. It is useful for teaching us what is true. It is useful for correcting our mistakes. It is useful for making our lives whole again. It is useful for training us to do what is right. By using Scripture, a man of God can be completely prepared to do every good thing." The verse tells us that the Bible is useful and prepares us for each day of our life. The Bible is God's guidebook for life. I want to encourage each of you to read your Bible to learn more about what God is like and how much He loves us. Let's pray.

Prayer: Thank You, God, for the Bible. And thank You, God, for speaking to us through the Bible.

Application Activity: Bible Sharing Game

Materials Needed: Strips of paper and a paper bag
Challenge: Memorize this week's memory verse and share it with a friend.

Have the children come up with their own reasons why the Bible is the most important book. See if they can list ten reasons that the Bible is important.

Family Moment

Share some of your favorite Bible verses with one another. Consider, beginning today, memorizing and learning one new Scripture verse a week as a family.

6. Jesus Grew Up Like You

Scripture Verse: Luke 2:52

Verse to Memorize: Luke 2:52

Missional Lesson: Children will learn about the early life of Jesus.

Message

Materials Needed: A tape measure.

(*Take a tape measure from your pocket.*) Today, I have brought a tape measure from home. We can measure many things with a tape measure to see how long and big they are. Hey, I've got an idea. Let's measure one of you. I need one volunteer. Who wants to be measured? (*Consider enlisting children and parents beforehand. Ask one of the children to stand up. Measure his or her height. Say the child's height. Then invite one of his or her parents to come forward. Measure the parent. Ask the parent to stay with the child.)*

As you can see, there is a big difference between *(child's name)* and his or her parent. However, we know that *(child's name)* is going to grow up and most likely be close to the height of one of his or her parents. The Bible tells us that Jesus grew just like you and me. We know from the Bible that Jesus grew in height. Also, the Bible says that Jesus grew in wisdom. Growing in wisdom is learning and understanding new things. Each year you learn new things in school. As you learn new things, you grow in knowledge. When you understand the thing you learned, that is wisdom.

Not only did Jesus have a good relationship with people, but also with God. We learn that Jesus prayed to God and studied Scripture. Doing these things helped Him to follow God daily and teach others about God. You can be like Jesus. As you grow up, you will learn to read and write similar to Jesus. However, it is up to you to be like Jesus when it comes to relating to other people and God. You can be like Jesus when you treat others like He would. And most importantly, you can be like Jesus when you read and follow what the Bible says. And you can be like Jesus by praying. Let's pray.

Prayer: God, as we grow each day, help us to be more and more like Jesus.

Application Activity: How Do I Grow?

Materials Needed: Paper and pencils
Challenge: Talk to God through prayer each day this week and ask Him to help you grow in height, wisdom, and stature as Jesus did.

Have each child make a measurement chart. Instead of inches, use ages. At each age, have the child write or draw something that he or she learned or did. Help the child fill in the chart with items like *started talking, started walking, got a baby brother, began preschool, learned to multiply, became a Christian,* etc. Have children discuss how they can be more like Jesus as they grow.

Family Moment

Discuss how each child grew and help them to put more things on their growth chart. Also, discuss and celebrate different milestones of your faith.

7. Jesus' Life on Earth

Scripture Passage: Luke 4:42–43

Verse to Memorize: Luke 4:43

Missional Lesson: Children will learn about the adult life of Jesus.

Message

Materials Needed: Toolbox and hammer

(*Have the toolbox open so children can see the items inside; remove harmful items.*) Hello, boy and girls. I brought my toolbox to church today. (*Take hammer from the box.*) This hammer reminds me of my friend Jesus. Did you know that Jesus built things? His father was a carpenter, and Jesus was a helper to his father. When He was an adult, He began a life of telling other people about God. He taught people about the kingdom of God, He healed the sick, and He performed many miracles. Many people believed Jesus and put their trust in God.

The Bible tells us that Jesus had disciples who followed Him. Wherever Jesus went, crowds would come to see Him and to hear Him teach. Jesus taught about how God wants us to treat others and told stories about the kingdom of God. Jesus showed love to the people that others didn't like. He welcomed children to come to Him and then He would hug them and pray for them.

We learn in the Bible that Jesus lived a perfect life and never sinned. We also learn in the Bible that Jesus obeyed God and spent time in prayer with Him. Jesus' life set a good example for us to follow. Let's close in prayer.

Prayer: God, thank You for Jesus and the life that He lived on earth. Thank You for the love He showed each of us.

Application Activity: Life of Jesus Timeline

Materials Needed: Signs with one verse per sign
Challenge: Create a timeline of Jesus' life.

Give each child a sign that represents an event in Jesus' life. If you have a large group, pair up two or more children with one sign or double the signs for a second timeline. Read the passages (out of order) to the children and have the children figure out the order of each event.

Consider limiting the number of verses used with younger children.

Jesus was born—Luke 2:11
Jesus' first visit to the temple—Luke 2:27

Jesus grew in wisdom and stature—Luke 2:40
Jesus was baptized—Luke 3:21–22
Jesus was tempted—Luke 4:1–2
Jesus began to teach—Luke 4:15
Jesus began to perform miracles—Luke 4:38–39
Jesus chose His disciples—Luke 5:8–11
Jesus sent out His disciples to preach and perform miracles—Luke 9:1–2
Jesus blessed the children—Luke 18:15–17
Jesus was arrested—Luke 22:54
Jesus was crucified—Luke 23:33–34
Jesus arose from the grave—Luke 24:4–6
Jesus told the disciple to go and tell others—Luke 24:46–49
Jesus went to heaven—Luke 24:51

Family Moment

Use the verses above to make a life of Jesus timeline. Discuss the significance of each of the events on the timeline.

8. The Holy Spirit

Scripture Passages: John 14:26; Galatians 5:22

Verse to Memorize: John 14:26

Missional Lesson: Children will learn about the Holy Spirit.

Message

Materials Needed: Photo of a friend

I brought a picture of one of my friends. *(Show the photo of your friend.)* *(Name of friend)* is my friend because we have fun doing things together. But more than that, *(name of friend)* is my friend because he is someone I can talk to, I can trust, and who cares about me.

In the Bible, Jesus tells His disciples that when He goes to heaven He will send a comforter (a friend), to take His place. Jesus kept His promise. After He died, came back to life, and went to heaven, the Holy Spirit came. The Holy Spirit is like having Jesus here. We learn in the Bible some of the things that the Holy Spirit does. He comforts us in times of trouble. He lets us know when we sin. He helps us make choices. He helps us understand the Bible. He helps us do God's work. And He helps us to be more like Jesus by helping us to be loving, joyful, peaceful, patient, kind, good, faithful, gentle, and to have control over ourselves. Let's pray, thanking God for the Holy Spirit.

Prayer: God, thank You for sending the Holy Spirit to help us be more like Jesus.

Application Activity: Magnetic Picture Frame

Materials Needed: 5-by-7 picture frames from card stock for every child, strip magnets, and markers or crayons
Challenge: Read Galatians 5:22 every morning this week. Pray that the Holy Spirit will help you show loved, joy, peace, patience, kindness, goodness, faithfulness, gentleness, and self-control.

Read Galatians 5:22. Explain that the verse teaches us how the Holy Spirit help us to be loving, joyful, peaceful, patient, kind, good, faithful, gentle, and to have control over ourselves. Cut 5-by-7 picture frames from card stock for each child. On one side, write at the top *The Holy Spirit helps me* . . . On the other side glue a magnet to the top of the frame.

Give each child a picture frame. Ask each child to write on the frames how the Holy Spirit helps us to act (as stated in Gal. 5:22). With younger children, have this prepared beforehand. After the children have finished the words, have them decorate their frames. Encourage children to take their frames home, tape a picture of themselves in it, and stick the frame on the refrigerator.

Family Moment

Discuss Galatians 5:22 and brainstorm ways the Holy Spirit might help someone to act out each characteristic.

9. Peter

Scripture Passage: Acts 2:37–39

Verse to Memorize: Acts 2:38

Missional Lesson: Children will learn about Peter and how the Holy Spirit gave him courage to tell about Jesus.

Message

Peter was one of Jesus' disciples. He was a very close friend to Jesus. Peter taught about God and performed miracles with Jesus and the other disciples. However, when Jesus was arrested, Peter lied and told three people that he did not know Jesus. Many believe that Peter may have been afraid that if people found out he was a follower of Jesus that he too would be arrested. The Bible tells us that Jesus forgave Peter. Before Jesus went to heaven, He told Peter that God would send the Holy Spirit to help Peter and the disciples tell others about Him.

Peter and the other disciples waited. Then on the day called Pentecost the Holy Spirit came and Peter began to preach. The Holy Spirit gave Peter the courage to tell others about Jesus. The Bible said that over 5,000 people heard about Jesus and believed and trusted Him. Peter was so excited about Jesus that he begin traveling to different places to preach so that people might hear Jesus' story and be saved. Peter was one of the first missionaries. Let's pray.

Prayer: God, thank You for helping Peter to tell others about Jesus.

Application Activity: Case Study

Challenge: This week think of one way that you can tell someone about Jesus. Then take courage from God like Peter did and tell someone about Jesus.

Read the following case study:

Lydia has just moved to a new state. She begins a new school tomorrow. If you were her new neighbor, what would you tell Lydia to help her have courage?

Have the children discuss what courage is. Let them share examples of when they have been courageous. Discuss how Peter's courage came from being with Jesus and from the presence of the Holy Spirit.

Family Moment

Ask family members to share about a time when they were encouraged to do something that they were unsure of or afraid of. Parents, share how God has given you courage to stand for God.

10. The Disciples of Jesus

Scripture Passage: Luke 9:23; Matthew 26:17–30

Verse to Memorize: Luke 9:23

Missional Lesson: Children will learn about discipleship.

Message

Materials Needed: A picture of the Last Supper and a Bible

I want to share a picture with you. (*Hold up a picture of the disciples at the Last Supper.*) This is a picture of the people who followed Jesus. They are called disciples. When Jesus was on earth, He choose 12 men to follow Him and help Him do God's work. We read in the Book of Luke that Jesus told His disciples that if they wanted to follow Him, they must forget about themselves, take up their cross, and follow Him. Jesus was saying that they needed to be prepared to go through some tough times and be willing to do God's work no matter what happened.

Let's look at the picture again. This picture is often referred to as the Last Supper. This is the last day that all of the disciples were together with Jesus before He died. They had some tough times ahead. The next time we hear that the disciples are together is after Jesus comes back to life and appears to them. Jesus comes to them and they are so happy that He is alive. Then Jesus returns to heaven. At this point, the disciples wanted to tell everybody about Jesus.

What Jesus told His disciples in Luke 9:23 applies to us. *(Read Luke 9:23.)* If we want to follow Jesus, we must forget about what we want and focus on what God wants. Let's pray.

Prayer: God, I pray that it will become our desire daily to follow You.

Application Activity: Modern Disciples

Materials Needed: Ten pictures of people in your church ministering or serving
Challenge: Plan a ministry project this week to let someone know that Jesus loves him or her.

Have ten pictures of people serving in the church and ministering outside of the church. Ask the children to tell you how the people in each picture are forgetting about themselves and doing what God wants them to do.

Help children to create a ministry project they can do this week to help a neighbor. Ideas include picking up trash in the yard, taking cookies to new neighbors, sending an encouraging note, or reading a book to an elderly neighbor.

Family Moment

Plan and implement a family ministry project in your neighborhood such as visiting the neighbors, helping an elderly neighbor with yard work, etc.

11. Paul

Scripture Passage: Acts 9:1–25

Verse to Memorize: Acts 9:22

Missional Lesson: Children will learn how God transformed Paul's life and used him to start churches.

Message

Materials Needed: A map of the missionary journeys of Paul (found in the back of many Bibles)

I have a map that I want to show you. (*Show the children the map of Paul's journey.*) The lines you see on the map show the places a man named Paul traveled to tell people about Jesus.

Paul wasn't always excited about telling other people about Jesus. In fact, before he became a Christian, he was called by another name, Saul, and he hated Christians. He spoke out against the Christians who taught about Jesus' death and resurrection. He wanted them arrested and put to death. However, God had another plan for Saul. As Saul was traveling to the city of Damascus, God confronted Saul in a vision and asked him why he was persecuting Him. The Bible says that God struck him blind. Jesus told him to get up and go to Damascus and then He would tell Saul what to do. For three days Saul was blind. Then God sent a disciple called Ananias to Saul. Ananias laid his hands on Saul and Saul's sight was restored and the Holy Spirit came to him. Immediately, he believed in Jesus and was baptized

From that point on, Saul's life was totally different. His friends began calling him Paul. He began preaching and traveling to faraway places to tell all people about Jesus. He also encouraged others to tell about Jesus. He started many churches and wrote letters to churches encouraging them to obey God's Word and to continue to tell others about Jesus. He challenged Christians that living for Christ is the most important part of every day. Let's pray.

Prayer: God, thank You for changing Saul's life. And thank You for what You do in our lives, too.

Application Activity: Skit

Materials Needed: Paper and pen to write out a role play
Challenge: Read more about the life of Paul throughout the Book of Acts.

Read Acts 9:1–22. Have the children create a role play and let them take turns acting out the Scripture passage. Discuss how Saul must have felt when God spoke to him. Discuss how Ananias must have felt when God told him to go to Saul. Discuss how Saul's life changed.

Family Moment

Verse 22 says that Paul proved to others that Jesus was the Christ. Think about ways that you individually and as a family·can show others that Jesus is the Christ.

II.

Foundations of Missional Living

12. My Purpose

Scripture Passage: Jeremiah 29:11

Verse to Memorize: Jeremiah 29:11

Missional Lesson: Children will learn that they were created for a purpose.

Message

Raise your hand if you have ever wanted your parents to do something for you. For example, have you ever wanted your parents to take you to the park or maybe to the circus? (*Share a personal example.*) In a similar way, God wants us to do something for Him. He wants us to live a life that brings honor and glory to Him, and to share with others His greatness and plan of salvation. That is the purpose that God has for each of us.

He wants us to live out our purpose every day. He has given each of us different experiences and talents to help us to bring honor to Him and to teach others about Him.

Here is an idea to help you remember each day that God has a purpose for you. Put a note on a mirror that you look into each morning. On the note write, *God, what can I do for You today?* Let your note to yourself be a reminder that God has a purpose for you. Let's pray.

Prayer: God, thank You for giving each of us a purpose. I pray that You would help each one of us every day to live our life in a way that honors You and brings others to You.

Application Activity: Prayer Drawing

Materials Needed: A blank sheet of notebook paper for each child and pencils or crayons

Challenge: Begin each day this week by asking God what He would have you do that day. At the end of the day, write a sentence or a draw a picture describing how you honor God throughout the day.

Give the children a piece of paper and have them write or draw a prayer to God. In the prayer, have them ask God for daily help in using their experiences and talents to honor Him. Discuss with the children that honoring God means seeking Him and following the teachings of the Bible. Share with the children how you use your experiences and talents to honor God. Then have children share examples.

Family Moment

Discuss what it means to honor God and how your family can do things together to honor God. Examples may be ministry projects, studying the Bible together, praying together, etc.

13. Go Forward!

Scripture Passage: Exodus 14

Verses to Memorize: Exodus 14:15–16

Missional Lesson: Children will learn through the story of Moses how they can rely on God. They will also learn that they can minister to others in hard times.

Message

Materials Needed: Walking stick or a piece of wood similar to a staff

(*Show the children the walking stick you have in your hand.*) How many different ways could I use this stick? I want to tell you about a story in the Bible where God uses a staff, like this one, to help other people through a difficult situation. The story is found in Exodus 14.

The story begins with God telling Moses to go to Egypt to free the Israelites from slavery. (*Explain slavery if the children look puzzled or if they are younger children.*) Moses did what God said and we learn that after many hardships in Egypt, the Pharaoh finally frees the Israelite slaves. God led Moses and the Israelites out of Egypt into the desert near the Red Sea. The Egyptian army followed the Israelites. The Israelites could not cross the sea to get away from the Egyptian army.

When the Israelites saw the Egyptian army, they cried out to God. They said that God brought them to the desert to die. But, Moses tried to calm the Israelites. Then God spoke to Moses (v. 15), "'Why are you crying out to me? Tell the people of Israel to move on.'"

The Bible says that God commanded Moses to raise his staff and stretch out his hands. Moses followed what God said and the sea parted and the Israelites walked through the middle of the sea with walls of water on both their right and left side, yet the ground was dry. God saved the Israelites from the Egyptians. (*Read verse 31.*) They saw God's power and trusted Him.

(*Hold up the stick.*) Do you think that Moses could have parted the sea without his staff? It is just a piece of wood someone carved from a tree. Moses' ability to part the sea wasn't the staff. God was the power, and the staff was a simple tool for Moses. Because Moses followed what God told him, God kept His promise and saved the Israelites. God will do the same in our lives. God wants us to look to Him for help and He will give us the strength to live each day. Let's pray.

Prayer: Lord, help us to remember to look to You for guidance in all things. Help us to live each day in Your strength.

Application Activity: God's Strength Drawings

Materials Needed: Paper and markers
Challenge: This week when you hear about someone who is having a hard time, pray for that person and give him or her a word of encouragement.

Discuss difficult situations that children are in such as a bicycle accident, illness, divorce, cuts, broken bones, death of a family member, etc. Discuss how God can help give us strength in each situation to go forward with life.

Have children draw a picture representing a time in their life that they felt God help them through a situation. Write on artwork: *When the people saw the power of the Lord, they feared the Lord and put their trust in Him.*

Have children share pictures and discuss how God has given them strength in the past and how we can trust Him to give us strength for the future because He keeps His promises. Also, discuss how they can minister to other people in difficult situations.

Family Moment

Share needs that you have and pray for one another. Then share needs that family and friends have and pray for them to find strength in God.

14. Missions Lifestyle

Scripture Passage: Micah 6:3–8

Verse to Memorize: Micah 6:8

Missional Lesson: Children will learn that God has a way that He wants them to live.

Message

Materials Needed: A fork and three medium-size poster boards to display the three guidelines found in the message (treat people fairly; love others faithfully; and live God's way)

In the Book of Micah we learn that God has some guidelines as to how He wants His people to live. God gave these guidelines to help them to live a better life and to protect them from things that could hurt them. Do your parents have guidelines for your life?

(*Show a fork.*) For example, how many of you are required by your parents to eat with a fork at dinner? Raise your hand if you have this rule in your home. How many of you have parents who tell you not to play in the street? Why is that a good guideline?

In the Bible we see that there are different guidelines that God gave Israel to live by. When we follow God's guidelines, it shows Him how great we think He is, and it also shows those around us how great God is in our lives.

In Micah 6:8, God gives three guidelines that we can follow today. Read Micah 6:8. (*Hold up a sign for each guideline as you give explanation.*) First, God wants us to treat people fairly. That is a simple guideline, but it is sometimes hard to live out every day. Sometimes we may not want to wait for others or listen to what they have to say. However, this guideline says to be fair.

Second, God wants us to love others faithfully. God wants us to love others, but this guideline goes a step further asking that we be faithful in our love. That means that no matter what a person says or does, they can depend on you to love them. This can be very hard to do.

Third, this verse says that we need to live God's way. That means that God wants us to live for Him in all the things that we do. He wants us to spend time in prayer and in studying the Bible so that we can know Him better. And He wants us to follow His guidelines.

Now let's review. Please repeat after me. (*Hold up the signs as you repeat the guidelines.*) (1) Treat people fairly. (2) Love others faithfully. (3) Live God's way. Let's close in prayer.

Prayer: God, thank You for giving us guidance on how to treat people, love others, and obey You. I pray that we will remember daily how You desire for us to live.

Application Activity: Micah 6:8 Scenarios

Challenge: This week as you think about how you treat others, ask yourself if you are treating others fairly, loving others faithfully, and living God's way. Display for the children the three posters used in the message. Have children take turns acting out each of the following scenarios. After each scenario, ask the children if the scenario is demonstrating acting fair, loving others, and living God's way. Encourage children to discuss how they could act differently in each scenario.

Scenarios:
1. Sticking out your tongue.
Answer: No, not acting fairly or loving others.

2. Helping someone else.
Answer: Yes, loving others.

3. Listening during Bible story time.
Answer: Yes, acting fairly and obeying God.

4. Cheating from someone else's test paper.
Answer: No, not acting fairly.

5. Forgiving a friend when he or she has hurt you.
Answer, Yes, loving others.

6. Telling your friend that you don't want him or her to come to church with you.
Answer: No, not loving others or obeying God.

If time permits, have children make up scenarios.

Discuss how children can minister to other children who are being mistreated.

Family Moment

Discuss how you want your children to respond when other children are not treating them fairly and when someone they love hurts them. Teach your children to deal with bullies and peer pressure in God's way.

15. Obeying God

Scripture Passages: 1 John 5:3; Acts 5:29; Ephesians 6:1; Hebrews 13:17

Verse to Memorize: 1 John 5:3

Missional Lesson: Children will learn that God expects them to obey Him.

Message

Materials Needed: A list of house rules or chores

Boys and girls, today I brought a copy of some rules from home to share with you. *(Show a sample copy of a list of possible house rules. The list could include items like clean the table when you are finished eating, put your clothes in the dirty clothes basket, pick up your toys when you are finished playing, etc. Read four or five rules.)* Do your parents have rules? Do you obey your parents and follow the rules for your home?

When you obey your parents, it shows that you love them. In the same way, when we obey God, that shows love and honor to Him. In fact, the Bible says that love for God is to obey His commands and that His commands are not hard to obey. That means when we obey the teachings in the Bible, that is showing God how much we love Him.

In the Bible we learn God wants us to obey Him, our parents, and our leaders. When we obey as God asks, it brings Him honor. I am going to read three different verses and after each one I want you to tell me who God is telling us to obey.

(*Read the following verses: Acts 5:29 [God]; Ephesians 6:1 [Parents]; Hebrews 13:17 [Leaders].*)

I'm going to name some of the ways that we can obey God. Clap your hands twice when your hear one that you will try to do this week. Treat others fairly. Do what you parents ask. Read your Bible. Do your work at school. (*Name others that relate to your children.*) Let's start obeying God today. Let's pray.

Prayer: God, help us to remember and obey every day the things that we have learned from Your Bible.

Application Activity: Obedience Calendar

Materials Needed: Paper and markers for each child to make a calendar
Challenge: Do your best this week to obey the commands that you have listed on your calendar.

Discuss with the children ways they can obey God this week. Make a calendar for the month. Have the children choose one or two ways they will try to obey God each week of the month. Have them write their choices on the calendar.

Family Moment

Parents, consider leading your whole family to participate in the application activity and developing a family calendar. Plan a family time during the week to talk about how hard or easy it was to follow the commands.

16. The Greatest Commandments

Scripture Passage: Matthew 22:37–40

Verse to Memorize: Matthew 22:37–38

Missional Lesson: Children will learn that God wants them to love Him and others.

Message

Materials Needed: A heart-shaped piece of poster board with *love* written on one side and *heart, soul,* and *mind* on the other side.

Boys and girls, today I'm going to talk about the first and greatest commandment. *(Show the children the heart with the word* love *on it.)* Jesus says in Matthew that the first and greatest commandment is to love the Lord with all your heart, soul, and mind. *(Turn the heart over to reveal the words* heart, soul, *and* mind.) The heart, soul, and mind represent all of you. Jesus is saying that God wants you to love Him with everything that you are and have.

Tell me some of the things that you love. *(As several of the children share, say after their statements,* God wants you to love Him more.) God wants us to love Him more than anything else in this world.

Jesus says the second most important command is to love your neighbor as you love yourself. This means that Jesus wants each of us to love the people around us just as much as we love ourselves. Part of loving others is being a friend and helping them when they need something.

Remember, when you love God first, it is easier to love others. And when we love others, it shows God that we love Him because we are obeying His commands. Let's pray.

Prayer: God, help us to love You with all that we are. And help us to love others better.

Application Activity: Love Notes

Materials Needed: A notecard for each child and markers or crayons

Challenge: This week write a love note to God every day. In each note, ask God to help you love others.

Have each child write or draw a picture representing a love note to God. The title should read "Dear God, I love You . . .". Let the children fill in the rest with their thoughts and imagination. Remember, these notes are the children's personal reflections of God.

Next have the child write or draw a friendship note to a friend or neighbor. The title should read "You are my friend and I love you." Write Matthew 22:39 on the note.

Family Moment

Have each family member share about loving God. Have each person in the family write or draw a love note to one another.

17. Talents and Abilities

Scripture Verse: 1 Corinthians 10:31

Verse to Memorize: 1 Corinthians 10:31

Missional Lesson: Children will learn that God gives them abilities to serve and honor Him.

Message

I want to share with you something that I like to do and can do pretty well. (*Share with the children a talent that you have. If possible, give them an illustration such as playing a musical instrument, spinning a basketball, drawing, etc.*) Take a moment and think of some of the things that you like to do and do well. Some kids like to play sports, while others like to play a musical instrument or sing. Some kids like to write stories while other like to draw pictures. We all have different things that we are good at doing and like to do. The things you are good at doing and like to do are called talents.

The Bible says that God gives us talents and wants us to use them to teach others about Jesus. (*Give specific examples of people in the church who use their talents for God. Ask children to think about ways they can use their talents for God.*) Let's close in prayer.

Prayer: God, thank You for giving me talents to share with others about You.

Application Activity: Talent Show

Challenge: Use your talents to honor God this week.

Ask the children to sit in a circle on the floor. Have children discuss different things they are good at. If a child feels that he or she is not good at anything, encourage the other children to tell that child what talents they see in her or him.

Have each child pick one talent and share with the group why he or she likes to do the talent. After each child shares, let the group brainstorm ways that child could use his or her talent for God.

Family Moment

Discuss how each person in the family has different talents. Think of some ways each talent brings honor to God. Consider planning a family ministry project based on the talents of the family. Be creative!

18. Working Together for God

Scripture Verse: 1 Corinthians 12:27

Verse to Memorize: 1 Corinthians 12:27

Missional Lesson: Children will learn that God has a plan for the people of the church to work together.

Message

Materials Needed: A packet of Kool-Aid®, a clear pitcher with water, a spoon, and one cup of sugar

In the Bible, God gives us an example of how He wants Christians to work together. He says that He wants Christians to work together because each person has a special part in ministering to others. Let me help you understand this a little better. I have a pack of Kool-Aid. However, I cannot make Kool-Aid without some help. (*Have adult helpers sitting close to the group who can bring you the resources that you need as you call for them.*)

OK, I have one pack of Kool-Aid (without sugar). Can I make Kool-Aid from just this? No, I'm going to need some help. Does anyone have a pitcher of water that I can put the Kool-Aid in? Does anyone have a spoon that I can stir this with? OK, now I have Kool-Aid. Wait. There is something missing. (*Have someone bring a bag of premeasured sugar [perhaps the pastor, children's minister, or a church leader the children know]. Stir the ingredients together.*) Wow, now I have Kool-Aid.

I want to say thanks to everyone for helping me make this Kool-Aid. I could not have done this without your help. If someone did not provide the pitcher of water, the spoon, or the sugar, I could not make the Kool-Aid.

God wants all Christians around the world to work together just like we worked together to make the Kool-Aid. He wants Christians to do their part to minister to others. When Christians work together and do their part, more people will learn about Jesus. Let's pray.

Prayer: God, thank You for the church. And thank You for letting kids have a part in working together in Your church.

Application Activity: Puzzle

Materials Needed: An age-appropriate puzzle
Challenge: This week write a letter or draw a picture for people in your church thanking them for working together for God.

Choose a puzzle that is age appropriate for the group and that they can complete in less than five minutes. Divide the number of puzzle pieces equally among the children, except for one piece and one child. Ask that child to sit out of the activity, and tell the group that you need her or him to help you with something else. As the children work together to complete the puzzle, give the one child the one piece of the puzzle. Guide the children working on the puzzle as needed.

As they complete the puzzle, children will realize one piece is missing. Let the child who has the missing piece tell the group that he or she can help because he or she has the missing piece of the puzzle. Have that child complete the puzzle. Debrief the activity by talking about how each child worked together to complete the puzzle. And how *(the one child)* felt when she was unable to work with the other children. Ask the children how they felt when they realized they were missing one piece. Then have them share how it felt when *(the one child)* was able to complete the puzzle.

God wants Christians to work together just like we worked together on the puzzle.

Family Moment

Find out about the ministries and missions your church works with. Tell your children how your church is working with missions organizations. Discuss and implement ways your family can be a partner in missions with the church.

19. God Is Great!

Scripture Passage: Isaiah 12

Verse to Memorize: Isaiah 12:4

Missional Lesson: Children will learn that God wants them to tell others about His greatness.

Message

Materials Needed: The front page of a newspaper

(*Display the front page of a newspaper.*) Extra! Extra! Read all about it! God's got a message and He wants us to shout it.

The newspaper tells people what is happening in their community and the world. It communicates a message. God wants us to communicate His message by telling others about Him. What are some ways that we can tell others about Him? Perhaps we could put articles in a newspaper, we could do a TV ad, or we could put up posters around our neighborhood.

(*Read Isaiah 12:4.*) In Isaiah 12, God gives us instructions on how to tell others about Him. First, God wants us to talk to Him and thank Him for all the things He has done for us. This means that God wants us to talk to Him and tell Him how wonderful He is. This is called praising God. He wants us to spend time thinking about Him and worshipping Him. Second, God wants us to tell others those things that we are thankful for. This means that God wants us to let the people around us know we are thankful for what He has done in our lives. Third, God wants us to tell others how great He is. This means that God wants us to tell people around us how wonderful He is to us so that they may know how wonderful He is as well.

Here is an example of how we would apply the verse to our lives. In your prayers you may say, "Thank You, God, for loving me and listening to my prayers." Then you would spend time reflecting on the greatness of God and worshipping Him. After you spend time with God, you would share with someone, "I'm so thankful that God loves me and listens to me when I pray. God is great. I love Him so much. He has been so wonderful to me." The more time we spend with God, the more of God we have to share with others. Let's pray.

Prayer: God, thank You for giving me instructions on how to tell other about You. I will share with others how great You are to me.

Application Activity: Newspaper

Materials Needed: Paper and pencils or crayons
Challenge: Use the newspaper you created to tell two people about God's greatness.

Explain that a testimony is sharing with others about God and that they are going to create a newspaper front page to help them share their testimony. Have children create a front page by answering the following questions, using pictures or writing. Have younger children draw their answers to the following questions.

What are you thankful for that God has done in your life?
How would you tell others about what God has done in your life?
How can you let others know about the greatness of God?

Family Moment

As a family, make a scrapbook or some scrapbook pages telling the story of God's presence in the life of your family. Consider using a newspaper motif.

20. I Can Do All Things Through Christ

Scripture Verse: Philippians 4:13

Verse to Memorize: Philippians 4:13

Missional Lesson: Children will learn that God promises they can do all things through Christ.

Message

Boys and girls, I want to say a Bible verse and then I want you to repeat after me. (*Read Philippians 4:13, then have the children repeat the verse after you.*) The Bible says that we can do all things through Christ Who gives us strength. Does that mean that you can pick up (*choose something in the room that would be impossible for a children to pick up*)?

God can do miracles, but I'm not sure that is what He wants us to learn from this verse.

This verse means that Christ Jesus will give you everything you need to do what God wants you to do. Listen to that sentence again. Jesus will give you everything you need to do what God wants you to do. So, do you think God wants you to lift that *(item stated above)*? No, but it does mean that Jesus will give you the strength you need to help you through times when you may be scared, sad, ill, angry, alone, hurt, or disappointed. He will give you strength you need when you don't have things you need or are away from people you love. He will give you strength to tell others about Jesus. Whatever the situation, Jesus will give you the strength you need. Remember that you can do all things through the power of Jesus Christ. *(Repeat Philippians 4:13. Then have the child repeat after you.)* Let's pray.

Prayer: God, thank You for promising to do all things through the power of Jesus.

Application Activity: All Things Responsive Reading

Materials Needed: Paper and pencils or crayons
Challenge: Display your "I Can Do All Things Through Christ" flyer in your room and each day this week add new things that you can do through Jesus Christ.

After each of the following sentences, have the children say, "I can do all things through Christ Jesus."

I can pray.
I can learn Scripture.
I can help others.
I can obey my parents.

I can share.
I can clean my room.
I can study for math.
I can tell others about Jesus.

Have the children make an 8½-by-11 flyer displaying all the things that they can do through Christ. Title the flyer, "I Can Do All Things Through Christ."

Family Moment

Discuss with your children some of the things that make you dependent on God. Pray with your child for some of the specific needs of your family.

21. Be an Example

Scripture Verse: Colossians 3:23

Verse to Memorize: Colossians 3:23

Missional Lesson: Children will learn that God wants them to be a good example to others.

Message

Materials Needed: A pencil, a textbook, a dustpan, a softball, sheet music, a picture of a missionary, a pet collar, a toy, and a Bible (Place everything in a pillowcase.)

Boys and girls, God wants us to be a good example to other. What are some ways that we can be a good example to others? In the Bible, Paul writes to the church in Colosse telling them, "Work at everything you do with all your heart. Work as if you were working for the Lord, not for human masters." For us, this means that God want us to do our very best every day in all that we do just as if He was the One Who asked us to do it. When we do things the best that we can, other people notice. And when they say, "You are doing a great job," you can tell them that you are doing it for God.

(Hold up the pillowcase.) In this bag I have a variety of things. I am going to show you something from the bag, and then I am going to tell you something that I can do related to the item I show you. After I finish my statement, I want you to say, "I can do my best for God." Let's practice. When I point in your direction, say, "I can do my best for God." Great. Let's begin.

Pencil—When I do my homework . . .

Textbook—When I study for a test . . .

Dustpan—When I sweep the floor . . .

Softball—When I play games . . .

Sheet music—When I sing . . .

Picture of a missionary—When I learn and support missions . . .

Pet collar—When I take care of pets . . .

Toy—When I play with others . . .

Bible—When I read my Bible . . .

Pillowcase—When I make up my bed . . .

Can you see that everything you do throughout the day can be done for God? This includes the things we don't think relate to God. Everything we do in life directly relates to God. God cares about every part of our day. Let's pray and thank God that He cares about all the things we do. Let's pray.

Prayer: God, thank You for caring about all the things we do or say. We pray that in all we do, we will do it as if we are working for You.

Application Activity: Pantomime

Materials Needed: Ten strips of paper and pencils or crayons
Challenge: This week as you are doing your chores, say a short prayer thanking God that He cares about everything you do.

Write the statements found after the list of items in the bag on ten separate strips of paper. Then give each child one statement and have them silently pantomime the activity in front of the group. Have the class guess what the child is pantomiming. Have the class create additional activities as time permits.

Discuss that how we do each of these activities matters to God.

Family Moment

Make a list of chores that the family can divide among the members. Encourage each family member to do the chore this week as if they were working for God and not Mom and Dad. With the family, compare how the house looked before and after. Explain how it is better when we do things for God.

22. The Great Commission

Scripture Verse: Matthew 28:19

Verse to Memorize: Matthew 28:19

Missional Objective: Children will learn about the Great Commission.

Message

Materials Needed: One sheet each of red, yellow, and green paper

In Matthew 28:19, Jesus says to His disciples (*read Matthew 28:19*). Jesus told His disciples to go and tell others about Him and teach what He had taught them. The disciples followed this verse and began to tell others. That is why we know about Jesus today. Jesus wants us to continue telling others about Him and the Bible's teachings.

I have an illustration to show you to help you in telling people about Jesus. (*Display the colored papers and begin the illustration.*) I have three pieces of paper in my hand—red, yellow, and green. What do these colors remind you of? (*Let the children guess until someone guesses a traffic light.*)

Yes, I was thinking of a traffic light. What does a red traffic light mean? (Stop.) What does a yellow traffic light mean? (Slow Down.) What does a green traffic light mean? (Go.)

Before Jesus went to heaven to be with God, He told His disciples to go! (*Hold up the green piece of paper.*) Jesus told His disciples to go to all the world. There are people we know and people we don't know in America and around the world who need to know Jesus.

Then He wants us to slow down (*hold up the yellow piece of paper*) and to know people so that we can tell them about Jesus. When people want to become Christians, we need to stop (*hold up the red piece of paper*) and teach them about Jesus until they are ready to go and tell others.

The next time you come to a traffic light, think about who you need to tell about Jesus. Let's pray.

Prayer: God, may we be reminded daily that You have asked us to go and tell others about Jesus.

Application Activity: Practicing the Great Commission

Materials Needed: Use the red, yellow, and green paper from the message.

Challenge: Teach someone in your family something that Jesus taught you.

Hold up the green piece of paper and ask the children where we are to go to tell others about Jesus. Tell them to be specific in their locations. After a few children have answered, hold up the yellow piece of paper. Ask the children how we can get to know people. Again, tell the children to be specific in their answers. After a few moments, hold up the red piece of paper. Ask the children what we tell people who are ready to become a Christian. You may need to help them understand the importance of each step (believe in Jesus, confess our sins, and obey God's Word).

Family Moment

This week tell your children about a missionary you know or one your church or denomination supports. Tell how the missionary teaches others the things that Jesus taught.

23. Different, But the Same

Scripture Verse: Genesis 1:27

Verse to Memorize: Genesis 1:27

Missional Lesson: Children will learn that all people are made in God's image.

Message

Materials Needed: A hand mirror, an adult, and a staff volunteer

(*Recruit an adult to sit beside you to assist with the illustration.*) Today my friend *(friend's name)* is going to help me. *(Friend's name)* and I are going to look in the mirror to see how alike we are. We each have a nose, two ears, and ten fingers. And what you cannot see is that we both have the same color blood and the same organs in our bodies.

Well, it looks like we are the same in many areas. I need help from one of the staff (*call on one of the staff persons*). Can you look at us and tell us how we are different? (*Let the staff volunteer describe three or four differences.*)

Wow, you are right. We have many differences, but we have many similarities. You know, it is the same way all over the world. God created every person in His image. All people have similarities, yet they have many differences. People around the world think differently, speak different languages, like different foods, and believe different things; but it is the same God Who created each person.

Jesus set an example for us to follow on how to treat people who are different from us. Jesus told us that He wants us to treat others just like we treat Him. Let's pray.

Prayer: God, help me to treat people who are different from me just like I would treat You.

Application Activity: Brainstorming

Challenge: This week make a friend with someone who is different from you.

Encourage children to share aloud ways that God would want them to treat the following persons:

Someone in a wheelchair
Someone much older
Someone who speaks a different language
Someone who believes in a different religion
Someone from a different ethnic background
Someone with a physical need

Share a personal story of how you or someone you know was blessed by meeting someone who was different from you or your friend.

Family Moment

Talk about the people in your community you see who are different from you. Discuss ways you can befriend people who are different from your family.

24. I Can Help Others

Scripture Passage: Matthew 25

Verse to Memorize: Matthew 25:35–36

Missional Lesson: Children will learn that they can do missions through helping others.

Message

Materials Needed: Teddy bear and a couple of toiletry items

Did you know that Jesus wants you to help others? (*Read Matthew 25:35–36.*) What are some ways we can help others? We can collect items like food, clothing, and toys to give to others. (*Display the teddy bear.*) One group of children collected teddy bears to give a local fire station. Each bear had an encouraging note attached. The firemen would give them to children to calm their fears when there was a fire.

(*Display the toiletry items.*) Other children have collected toiletry items to give to people who are homeless. (*Tell of additional ministry projects in which your church has participated.*)

No matter how young or old you are, you can help others. As children you can participate in ministry projects at church, at home, or you can create your own project. You can do ministry projects in a group or by yourself. When you see someone who needs help, think of some ways that you can help them. As you are helping them, share with them the love of Jesus. Let's pray.

Prayer: God, show me how I can help others.

Application Activity: Children's Activity Bags

Materials Needed: Several resealable quart-size plastic bags, pencils, colored paper, games, books, small toys, and crayons to give to children in need
Challenge: Help two people in need this week.

Gather supplies and resealable plastic quart bags to make activity bags for children in crisis. Supplies could include crayons, coloring sheets, novelty games, jacks, and a travel ticktacktoe board. Have the children divide the supplies and put them in the quart-size bags. Then have each child write a personal note with the Scripture verse to place inside the bag. Later, take the bags to a hospital waiting room, police station, fire station, domestic violence shelter, or child protective service for workers to give to children in crisis.

Family Moment

Volunteer at a soup kitchen or missions center. Debrief your experience afterwards.

25. I Can Pray for Other Christians

Scripture Verse: Matthew 9:37–38

Verse Memorize: Matthew 9:37

Missional Lesson: Children will learn that they can pray for missions.

Message

Materials Needed: Pictures of Christians in another country worshipping God, missionaries on the field, and of an unreached people group (*Get pictures from your church or mission board or go online to search for picture or resources; see resources on p. 177.*)

There are people all over the world who need to know about Jesus. (*Show picture of Christians in different countries worshipping God.*) In some countries there are many Christians. In other countries, there are very few Christians. In many countries there are missionaries. (*Show a picture of a missionary.*) Missionaries are people who go to another people or country to tell others about Jesus. The Christians that live in these countries and the missionaries work together to tell others about Jesus and to start churches.

We can support Christians in other countries and missionaries through our prayers. We can pray that Christians will be given the opportunity to minister to others and show the love of Jesus. We can pray that missionaries will help these Christians to start churches where people can worship. We can pray that missionaries will go places where there are no Christians. (*Show the picture of an unreached people group.*) We can pray that Christians around the world will work with one another so that everyone will have the opportunity to know Jesus. We can pray that when people hear about Jesus, they will believe and become Christians. Let's pray.

Prayer: God, we pray for the people of the world that do not know Jesus. We pray that Christians will go and tell these people about You.

Application Activity: Prayer for the World

Materials Needed: A world map and information about different countries around the world (See resources on p. 177.)

Challenge: This week at every meal pray that missionaries will go and tell others about Jesus.

Read Matthew 9:37–38. Explain that Jesus is describing the people who are ready to hear about Jesus as a field ready to be harvested. And Jesus wants us to pray that Christians would be willing to go and tell those who have never heard. Point to a country on the world map. Share with the children what you know about that country. Then guide children to have a quiet time and pray for that country using the following prayer list.

___ Pray for the Christians in the country.

___ Pray for the non-Christians in the country.

___ Pray for missionaries who are serving in that country.

___ Pray that Christians around the world will be willing to go and teach about Jesus.

Repeat the process with another country as time allows.

Family Moment

Adopt a missionary family to pray for. If possible, contact the missionaries and ask for specific prayer requests (see resources on p. 177).

26. I Can Learn About Missions

Scripture Passage: Isaiah 52:1–10

Verse to Memorize: Isaiah 52:10

Missional Lesson: Children will learn that missions is the story of what God is doing in the world.

Message

Materials Needed: A globe

In my hand, I have a globe. This globe represents the whole world. When I tell you stories about missionaries or about Christians from different parts of the world, I am telling you a mission story. Through missions, I am telling you what God is doing around the world.

Every day God is working in the world through people and situations to teach all nations about Him. It is God's desire that all the nations, people, and tribes of the world come to learn about Him and hear of how great and glorious He is. Through television, radio, and the Internet, we hear about what is happening in the world daily. All around the world there are small groups of Christian in these places doing ministry and sharing the love of God. These Christians, nationals and missionaries, need our support.

Here are two things we can do to support them. Number one, when you hear about countries in the news, pray for the Christians and missionaries in that country. And number two, seek to learn more about missionaries, ministries, and people groups. In our church, we have (*share about the missions resources your church has to offer to help children and families learn about missions. These could include library resources, classes, information about missionaries your church supports, families of missionaries, etc.*).

It is through learning about missions that we are able to learn what God is doing in the world. Also, missions helps us to see the needs of the people around us. Let's pray.

Prayer: God, help us to learn more about missions. Help us to support Christians in our communities and around the world so that they can tell others about You.

Application Activity: Missionary Profile

Materials Needed: Collect information from your church to make missionary profile cards, several index cards, pencils, and poster boards.

Challenge: This week use the missionary profiles to pray for a different missionary each day. Also, write the missionary a note of encouragement.

Divide children into groups of three to four. Give each group a missionary profile. Develop a missionary profile from information you obtain through missionaries your church or denomination supports. The profile should include: name and family members names *(in some high-security areas names may need to be changed)*, country, type of work, home state, email address *(if possible, list a way that the children may contact the missionary)*, and birthday. Then have children create a play, song, poem, or poster to share with the other children about the information they have been given.

Allow the children to share their creative interpretations. Then lead the children to pray for each of the missionaries. Give each child a copy of the missionary profiles to take home.

Family Moment

Take one of the missionary profiles and do some research on the country and the people where the missionaries minister. Use a library, bookstore, or the Internet to gather your research. Lead your family to pray for the missionary and send a word of encouragement to the missionary.

27. I Can Give to Support Missions

Scripture Passage: 2 Corinthians 8:1–7

Verse to Memorize: 2 Corinthians 8:5

Missional Objective: Children will learn that they can give to support missions and will learn how missionaries are supported.

Message

Materials Needed: A box with a slit in the lid

I have a box with a slit in the top of it. What do you think this is? Yes, it is sort of like a bank. In the late 1800s, when people traveled by horse and buggy, groups of children in church would have boxes like these that they called mite boxes. (A mite is the smallest Jewish coin in

Jesus' time.) What do you think they did with these boxes? Yes, that is correct. They collected coins throughout the week and gave the money to support missionaries.

Today missionaries still do missions through the financial support they receive from children and adults in churches. There are basically two ways that missionaries are supported. One is called faith-based missionary support where missionaries ask for support from churches and individuals. The other way missionaries are supported is through the giving of many churches. These churches put their money together and give it to a board that sends out missionaries. That board divides the money among all their missionaries to support the missionaries' ministries. Some missionaries are partially supported by cooperative giving, yet may have to raise a portion of their support.

No matter how you look at it, missionaries need our support. It is the support from individuals and churches that keep missionaries on the missions field. (*In five sentences or less, share about how your church supports missionaries.*)

Boys and girls, I want you to think about the missionaries you know. And this week I want you to save your extra coins and bring them to church next week. (*Specify when and where the children need to put their coins. If you do not do the application activity with the children, consider giving each child a box to put their change in.*) Let's close in prayer.

Prayer: God, thank You for the things that You give us. I pray that we will remember daily that missionaries need our support and that we will give what we can to support them.

Application Activity: Mite Box

Materials Needed: A small gift box for each child, tape, stickers, and markers or crayons
Challenge: This week collect money that you save or make and set aside one-tenth for a tithe. Give the rest to missions.

Discuss the memory verse and the importance of tithing to the church and giving above the tithe to support missions.

Have the children make mite boxes out of small gift boxes. Cut a slit in the top of the box and then have the children tape the box together and decorate it with stickers and markers. Encourage the children to take the box home and use it to collect change to give to missions.

Family Moment

Discuss giving to missions and develop a family plan to support missions.

28. I Can Do Missions

Scripture Verse: 2 Corinthians 5:20

Verse to Memorize: 2 Corinthians 5:20

Missional Lesson: Children will learn that they can do missions.

Message

Last week I asked you to save your extra coins and bring them to church this week. If you brought your coins, put them in (specify a location to collect the coins). We will send this money to help the missionaries. Thank you for giving.

Today I have a special message for you. The Bible says in 2 Corinthians 5:20 that God wants us to be His ambassadors. Raise your hand if you know what the word *ambassador* means. Let me give you an example of an ambassador. Other countries have ambassadors that travel to neighboring countries to speak for their home country. For example, America has an ambassador that lives in Spain. The American ambassador speaks for the American government to the Spanish government. In the same way, God wants Christians to be ambassadors for Him each day that we live. Missionaries choose to be ambassadors for Christ by crossing cultural boundaries to minister to people. They often have to move to a new location.

However, God isn't just talking about missionaries living in another country. He is talking about every Christian. God has called many Christians to live in other countries, but He has also called people to stay where they are and do missions where they currently live. There are people around us every day who may need to know Jesus, who need a church family, who need a friend, who need help with bills or tasks, who need transportation, who need food, or who need a Bible. We need to take time and be an ambassador for Christ to them. We need to be like Jesus to these people by meeting their needs, loving them, and helping them to become a Christian. Let's pray and ask God to help us be ambassadors for Jesus to our community.

Prayer: God, help us to represent You each day of our life and to minister to people as You would.

Application Activity: Ambassador's Pledge

Materials Needed: Paper and pencils
Challenge: Each morning review the pledge and at the end of the day write the ways that you fulfilled your pledge.

Have children brainstorm ways that they can be ambassadors for Christ in their community through doing missions. Then give children a piece of paper and ask them to write five ways that they will try to be an ambassador for Christ. If the children are nonreaders, have them draw two ways they can be an ambassador for Christ. Have each child make up a personal pledge using the ideas they created.

Let children share their pledges with the class.

Family Moment

Create a family pledge by listing ways your family will be ambassadors for Christ in your home and community.

III.
Foundations of Missions

29. Why Be a Missionary?

Scripture Passage: 2 Corinthians 5:14–15

Verse to Memorize: 2 Corinthians 5:15

Missional Lesson: Children will learn why people become missionaries.

Message

I have some pictures of missionaries to show you. These are missionaries that our church supports. (*Share about one and a half minutes about the missionaries and where they are serving. Write out what you are going to say ahead of time.*)

Christians become missionaries because they feel that is what God has asked them to do. God wants us all to tell about Jesus. He asks some people to give up their life as they know it and move to a different place, or to minister to people who are different from them.

Paul tells us in 2 Corinthians 5:14 that it is the love of Jesus that causes us to go to a different place and a different people to tell them about Jesus. As with all missionaries, it is the love of Jesus that makes them want to be a Christian. And it is the love of Jesus that makes them want to go and tell others.

Often, becoming a missionary means moving and living in a community or country that is very different from their hometown. The missionary families must take time to learn about the differences and similarities of the people they will be living among. And they will have to change the way they live to fit into the new place. Plus, they sometimes have to learn a different language just to be able to talk to the people in their new community. Missionaries' kids (MKs) have to adjust to a different home, neighborhood, and school. Sometimes MKs attend home school or an international school. Others may have to attend boarding school away from their parents.

Being a missionary requires many changes. However, missionaries go into missions trusting that God will take care of all their needs. Let's pray.

Prayer: God, I thank You for sending Christians out as missionaries and for working in their lives.

Application Activity: Brainstorm

Materials Needed: Paper and pencil or crayons
Challenge: Write a letter to a missionary.

In the Book of Ruth, we see God use Ruth to go to a different people and live among them. Ruth had to change the way she lived. It was difficult for Ruth in the beginning, but God blessed Ruth for obeying and being faithful to Him.

Brainstorm some things that missionaries give up. Lead children to talk about leaving family, friends, restaurants, foods, school, neighborhood, etc.

Brainstorm some things that missionaries gain. Lead children to discuss new friends, learn about a different people, learn a different language, see new places around the world, etc. Also, consider showing pictures you may have of the region where missionaries are serving and have the children describe how some of the things are the same or different than they are used to.

Close by having each child write a note or draw a picture giving thanks to the missionary for following God and doing missions.

Family Moment

Assemble and send a care package to a missionary family.

30. What Do Missionaries Do?

Scripture Verse: Romans 10:15

Verse to Memorize: Romans 10:15

Missional Lesson: Children will learn the basics of how missionaries work.

Message

I want to tell you about what missionaries do. God tells us all to go to all nations and make disciples. The job of the missionary is to go and to teach others about God, Jesus, and the Holy Spirit. Say, "Go and teach" with me.

Missionaries go and teach in many different ways. Some missionaries go and take care of physical needs like providing food, clothing, health care, and education to help people have a better life. However, as these missionaries help people, they also tell the people that they are there because God has sent them to help them. People learn about Jesus through the compassion of the missionaries.

Some missionaries go and live and work among people to build friendships. Through these new friendships, the people begin to study the Bible and often become Christians. Through friendships, missionaries share about Jesus and people become Christians. Then the new Christians begin telling others about Jesus. In many cases new churches are begun.

Some missionaries go and have big rallies or hand out information about Jesus on the streets. They share the story of Jesus with strangers. These strangers hear the story of Jesus and many believe and become Christians.

Missionaries could use the ways that I told you about or many other ways. They use different ways to reach different people. No one way is better than another. The important thing is that missionaries go and teach others about God, Jesus, and the Holy Spirit. Let's pray.

Prayer: God, help the missionaries around the world to go and teach about You.

Application Activity: Missionary Case Study

Materials Needed: A picture of the Olympics, a picture of an apartment complex, a picture of the homeless, three pieces of poster board, and markers or crayons
Challenge: This week make time to pray for missionaries who minister to people at the Olympics, to people who live in apartment complexes, and to people who are homeless.

Today we are going to develop a strategy for doing missions. I am going to divide you into three groups and give each group a situation. I want each group to come up with a way that missionaries will tell others about Jesus. (*Write these on a sheet of paper or have pictures that represent each characteristic. Let the children be creative by drawing their answers on a poster board. Then let them share with the other children.*)

Olympics
Apartment complex
Homeless

Possible answers:
Olympics—Give out water, give out Olympic trading cards, etc.
Apartment complex—Live at the apartment complex, provide sports activities to the children after school, tutoring, make friends, etc.
Homeless—Provide food and shelter, collect clothes or blankets, etc.

Family Moment

Research the ministries in your community. As a family, volunteer to work one day at the ministry of your choice.

31. Families Doing Missions Together

Scripture Passage: 1 John 3:18

Verse to Memorize: 1 John 3:18

Missional Lesson: Children will learn that they can do family missions projects.

Message

Materials Needed: Collect items representing places the children would go for vacation (i.e., the beach, the mountains, a dude ranch, etc.)

I have some items I want to show you today. (*Show the children some items that symbolize where the majority of the children may vacation. The goal is to have the children recognize items they use on vacation. If the majority of the children vacation at the beach, use items such as a beach ball, suntan lotion, a camera, suitcase, sunglasses, and a swimsuit.)*

Where do you think I would use these items? (On vacation.) Yes, these are items that I might use on vacation. Every year families just like yours give up a traditional vacation to go on a missions trip. How many of you would be willing to give up going on vacation to go on a missions trip?

One family missions experience is called FamilyFEST℠. The FamilyFEST experiences puts families with children first grade and up to work ministering to others around the United States. Children participate alongside a parent in such ministries as block parties, Backyard Bible Clubs, painting, etc.

We may not all be able to attend FamilyFEST, but we can as families do ministry projects in our own community and even in other communities when we travel to share the love of Jesus. No matter where we go, there are always people around us who need to know about Jesus. Let's pray.

Prayer: God, we thank You for the families that participate in FamilyFEST. Help us as a church family to minister to those in our community.

Application Activity: Family Missions Word Play

Materials Needed: One piece of poster board, paper cut in strips, three large bags, and masking tape
Challenge: Each day this week pray for families serving overseas as missionaries and families participating on missions trips together.

Before the activity, write on the outside of the three large bags *Place*, *Ministry*, and *Packing List*. Write each of the items listed below on an individual strip of paper. Then sort the strips into the appropriately labeled bag. Put the names of a location in the *Place* bag, put the types of ministry in the *Ministry* bag, and the list of ministry items in the *Packing List* bag.

Write on a poster board: *I'm going on a missions trip to _____ where I will be _____. I will be taking a _____ with me.*

Seattle, Washington
Surveying a neighborhood to invite people to church
Pencil, notebook, and an umbrella

San Diego, California
Teaching a Backyard Bible Club
Bible stories and games for children

Mountains of North Carolina
Working at a community block party
Face painting kit and balloons

New York City
Distributing food
A box of grocery bags

West Virginia
Painting a house
Paintbrush and ladders

Vancouver, Canada
Giving out information about Jesus
Coat and good walking shoes

Hawaii
Leading a Vacation Bible School
Sunglasses, shorts, and Bibles

Tell the children they are going to make up a sentence telling about a missions trip. Have one child draw one strip from each of the different bags. Tape the *Place* strip in the first blank line, the *Ministry* strip in the second blank line, and the *Packing List* strip in the third blank line. Then read the sentence. Remove the strips from the poster board. Repeat the steps with another child until all three bags are empty.

Then tell the children these are some of the ministries from FamilyFEST. Now let's see how they are really supposed to fit together. (*Guide the children to figure out which sentence strips go together. The answers are in the chart.*)

Family Moment

Consider sponsoring a churchwide family ministry project in your community.

FamilyFEST is a ministry of the Woman's Missionary Union. For more information about this ministry visit www.wmu.com/getinvolved/ministry/volunteer/projects.asp.

32. Missionaries' Kids (MKs)

Scripture Verse: Psalm 29:11

Verse to Memorize: Psalm 29:11

Missional Lesson: Children will learn about MKs and how they can support MKs through prayer.

Message

Materials Needed: Picture of MKs

Have you ever heard of a missionaries' kid (MK)? (*Show pictures of some missionary families that your church supports.*) MKs are children or teenagers whose parents serve as missionaries.

MKs have to adjust to a new way of life and often a new language just like their parents. MKs' lives are different based on where their parents are located. For example, schooling is different for each family. Some children go to a local school with children from their new community. Some go to an international school where English is spoken. Some leave home and go to boarding school with other MKs. And some kids are homeschooled. However MKs are educated, they must also adjust to many other changes like new friends, a new culture, a new home, new foods, new neighbors, and oftentimes a new language.

Many missionaries who work overseas return to the United States after working three to five years on the missions field. When MKs come back to the US, they have to readjust to life back here. The family and friends they knew before they left have changed; so MKs may feel that they don't fit in because they have been away for so long.

However, there are things that we can do to support MKs. One thing we can do is pray for them. Psalm 29:11 says, "The LORD gives strength to his people. The LORD blesses his people with peace." We can pray this verse for MKs. We can pray that as they adjust to new situations, they will know God's strength and peace. Another thing we can do is encourage them through emails and care packages. They will be encouraged knowing that someone is praying and caring for them. Another thing we can do is be a friend to MKs when they come home and help them fit into school, the church, and the neighborhood. Let's pray for MKs right now.

Prayer: God, thank You for MKs. We pray that they will feel Your strength and peace in all that they do.

Application Activity: MK Care Package

Materials Needed: A greeting card for each MK, boxes, supplies for a care package (music, movies, books, dried food mixes, gum, hats, purses, toys, etc.), wrapping paper, scissors, tape, paper for notecards, and MKs' addresses
Challenge: This week pray for your MKs every night. Pick out a Bible verse to say when you pray for them.

Ask the children if they enjoy getting something in the mail. Tell the children that MKs enjoy receiving things in the mail as well. (Check with MKs' families before collecting and sending items.) Have the children wrap the supplies individually and place them in the boxes. Then have all the children sign all the greeting cards. As the children work, talk to them about the MKs that will be receiving the care packages. When the packages are packed and ready to be mailed, have the children pray for the MKs who will receive the packages.

Family Moment

Invite a missionary family from your church to dinner and ask them to share about their missions experience. Play some games related to each family's culture. If possible, adopt a missionary family from your hometown to support through prayers and encouragement. Contact your church or a missions organization/board your church supports for information on missionaries.

33. Short-Term Missions Involvement

Scripture Verse: 1 Corinthians 2:1

Verse to Memorize: 1 Corinthians 2:1

Missional Lesson: Children will learn that people can support and do missions through short-term missions projects.

Message

I have some great news to share with you about missions. The news is that every year more and more people are doing short-term missions, partly because more people are able to travel. Short-term missions can be a one- or two-week missions trip, a ten-week summer missions trip, a three-month missions assignment, or a two-year or less volunteer missions trip. Because of the different short-term missions trips, more people are able to participate in missions. Plus, these volunteers help missionaries start new ministries and strengthen existing ministries.

The most popular of the short-term missions projects is the one- to two-week missions trip. People are able to take time away from their regular jobs to do missions. These projects vary. Projects include building churches, visiting neighborhoods, conducting Bible clubs for children, witnessing, doing musical performances, providing medical help, hosting block parties, working in missions centers, etc. *(Share in five to ten sentences a missions project in which someone from your church participated or about a future project.)* Let's pray.

Prayer: God, thank You that more people are able to do missions. I pray that You make a way for each one of us to be able to participate in missions in our lifetime.

Application Activity: My Missions Trip

Materials Needed: Paper and pencils or crayons
Challenge: This week think about the missions trip that you have created. Add things you might take with you to minister to people and help the missionaries.

Have children create a missions trip of their own by answering the following questions:
   What type of missions work would I do?
   Where would I go?
   How would I get there?
   Who would go with me?
   What would I take to give the people and missionaries?

Have the children share their missions trip with the other children.

Family Moment

Discuss as a family the possibilities of doing a short-term missions trip. Discuss what type of work you might be able to do together. Pray about how your family can be involved in short-term missions by supporting volunteers or going on a short-term missions trip.

34. Evangelism

Scripture Passage: Romans 10:14–15

Verse to Memorize: Romans 10:15

Missional Lesson: Children will learn that God wants people to tell others how to become a Christian.

Message

When I say the word *evangelism* what do you think of? Evangelism is telling someone about Jesus, telling them how they can become a Christian, and leading the person to become a Christian. Evangelism is done many different ways. You can share with one of your friends or you can share with someone you just met. It can be done one-on-one or with many people present. The best-known evangelist in the world is Billy Graham. Thousands of people come to hear him preach about how they can become Christians. Through his ministry, millions of people have heard about Jesus.

However, most evangelism happens by people just like you and me who want to share with others about Jesus and want others to have the opportunity to be a Christian. Romans 10:14 asks how people will hear about Jesus unless someone tells them. There are many people around the world and even people in our neighborhood who have never had anyone tell them about Jesus or about how to become a Christian. The verse goes on to say, "How beautiful are the feet of those who bring good news!" The good news the Bible is talking about is the good news about Jesus. (*In a fun way say the following question.*) Have you ever thought of your feet as beautiful? God is saying how beautiful it is to see Christians telling others about Jesus. Let's pray.

Prayer: God, it is a beautiful thing to tell others about Jesus and have them know and follow Him. Give us the courage to tell others about Jesus.

Application Activity: Philip and the Ethiopian

Materials Needed: Paper and pencils or crayons
Challenge: This week tell someone about Jesus.

Tell the children the story of Philip and the Ethiopian found in Acts 8:26–40. Ask the children to listen to the story and then to draw a picture about the story. Then ask them to share specific things that Philip did to share the good new of Jesus with the Ethiopian and how the Ethiopian responded.

Family Moment

If you are Christian, share with your child about how you became a Christian and who helped you learn about Jesus. If you are not Christians, read John 3:1–21 and discuss this story as a family. Pray about choosing to believe in Jesus, trusting Him to be the Lord of your life, and becoming a Christ follower.

35. Starting Churches

Scripture Passages: Ephesians 3:14–21 and Colossians 4:2–6

Verse to Memorize: Colossians 4:3

Missional Lesson: Children will learn about starting churches and how they can pray for these churches.

Message

Materials Needed: A textbook (or something representing a school) and movie ticket stubs

Hello, boys and girls. Today I brought two items with me. The first item is a schoolbook and the second item is a movie ticket. Can anybody tell me what these two things have in common? OK. It is a little hard to tell what these two things have in common. The answer I'm looking for is that many schools (*hold up the textbook*) and movie theaters (*hold up the ticket*) house new churches being started in North America. Groups of people meet in schools and movie theaters every Sunday to worship God and learn about Jesus. Churches are also being started in homes and apartments buildings or complexes. In fact, churches are being started around the world any place where small groups of people can come together and worship God. As you can see, a church, isn't just a building, it is the people that make up the church.

Starting a church is hard work. Many times missionaries are sent to places where there are no churches or any known believers. The missionaries begin by making friends. Then through the friendships, they start small-group Bible studies. Then through the Bible studies, the new friends become believers in Jesus and become Christians. These groups of new Christians begin meeting together to worship God. This is the beginning of a new church. This sounds pretty simple, but it isn't. Sometimes it takes three years or longer to get a church started.

The missionaries who start churches need our prayers. We can pray that they will make new friends in the community. We can pray that their new friends will want to learn more about Jesus and become Christians. And we can pray that a church will be started where more people will have an opportunity to worship God. I have a prayer that Paul spoke to God for the church at Ephesus. I would like to read that as our prayer today for our new churches around the world. Let's pray.

Prayer: (*Read Ephesians 3:14–21.*)

Application Activity: Pray for Missionaries and New Churches

Challenge: Write a church starter and ask what his or her work is like. Pray for this missionary daily.

Tell the children that many of the New Testament books are letters that Paul wrote to churches that he helped start. For example, Ephesians was a book written for the church at Ephesus; and Colossians was a book written to the church in Colosse. Read Colossians 4:2–6 to the children. Describe how this letter relates to churches today. Have the children spread out in the room and give them five minutes to have an individual quiet time for praying for new and established churches in the world. They can use the prayer examples in Ephesians 3:14–21 and Colossians 4:2–6.

If possible, give children specific missionaries, church names, and needs from church starters your church supports.

Bring the children together. Close by praying for the people of the world, that they may be given the opportunity to worship God.

Family Moment

Discuss the importance of belonging to a body of believers and having the opportunity to worship God together. Parents, tell your children your personal testimony of how you feel about being a part of a church.

36. Storying

Scripture Verse: Isaiah 55:11

Verse to Memorize: Isaiah 55:11

Missional Lesson: Children will learn about how missionaries are reaching people groups through chronological Bible storying.

Message

I want to show you some of the pages in my Bible. As you can see my Bible looks similar to the Bibles that you have in your homes. However, neither my Bible nor your Bible has always looked like this. In fact, from the beginning, the stories from the Bible were spoken from parent to child. As people began writing, they wrote the Bible stories on scrolls. When the printing press was invented, the Bible became available to many people. The first book printed was the Bible.

Today you can buy an English Bible at any bookstore in the US. However, there are many people in the world who don't know how to read or don't have the Bible translated into their language. One way that missionaries are teaching these people the Bible is through telling people the stories of the Bible and having them memorize the stories. Then the people memorize the stories of the Bible and tell others. This process is called chronological Bible storying. Many people around the world are becoming Christians because they are hearing the Bible being told in their language. Let's pray.

Prayer: God, thank You for the Bible and thank You that missionaries are translating the Bible and the stories of the Bible in a way that many people groups will learn about You.

Application Activity: Bible Story for Preschoolers

Materials Needed: Paper and pencils or crayons
Challenge: This week read a story in the Bible, and practice telling the story in a way that your friends can understand (older children can write out the story). Tell the story to someone.

For this particular application, we will focus on storytelling and have children actually take a story from the Bible and make it simple enough for a preschooler to understand. Have the children draw pictures that tell a Bible story. Then have the children practice telling the story with the pictures. Try to have an opportunity for the children to tell the story to a group of preschoolers.

Family Moment

Tell one of your favorite stories of faith from the Bible and discuss what the children learned from that story.

37. Becoming a Missionary

Scripture Verse: 1 Timothy 1:12

Verse to Memorize: 1 Timothy 1:12

Missional Lesson: Children will learn about how missionaries prepare to go to the missions field.

Message

Did you know that missionaries are trained before they go to the missions field? Missionaries must prepare for the work that God has asked them to do. Here are some ways that missionaries prepare. Missionaries are usually assigned to places that match what they are able to do. For example, if you are a farmer, you would most likely be sent to the countryside instead of a big city. Today, missionaries do many different jobs on the missions field: some teach English; some make videos; some coordinate handing out Christian literature, some work in orphanages or schools; some work with computers. In each of these jobs, missionaries are developing relationships and sharing the good news of Jesus.

So how do they prepare to go? Career missionaries may need to go to college or seminary to prepare to go to the missions field. After missionaries complete school, the mission board that supports them usually prepares them. They will learn things like how to teach the Bible to other people groups, how to live in a different culture, and ways to stay healthy. Missionaries may be required to attend language school when they are on the field. The mission board tries to prepare the missionaries for whatever situation arises.

After missionaries are trained, they usually are commissioned by a mission board or the church. A commissioning service is a time when the missionaries are prayed for and supported by their families and friends. A pastor gives a word of encouragement and inspiration for the missionaries and acknowledges the importance of their family and friends' support.

Then the missionaries are ready to go to the missions field. As the missionaries go, it is the responsibility of family and friends to pray for them and encourage them. Let's pray now for the missionary families.

Prayer: God, thank You for the missionaries, for the people who help prepare them, and for the friends and family that support them.

Application Activity: Create a Commissioning Service Message

Challenge: Each day this week pray for the new missionaries that are on the field.

Based on the information above, have the children develop ideas for a commissioning service message. Ask the children to brainstorm what the pastor might say to encourage missionaries and prepare them for mission service. Also have them brainstorm on what the pastor might say to encourage friends and family to support the missionaries. Write all of the children's ideas on a piece of paper. Then have the children think of Scriptures that would encourage the missionaries. Have a few of your favorite Scripture verses on hand to share.

Family Moment

Discuss some of the excitement and fear that missionaries must feel when they go to the missions field. Discuss how your family would adjust to different cultures.

38. Worldview

Scripture Verse: John 4:14

Verse to Memorize: John 4:14

Missional Lesson: Children will learn about biblical and
missional worldview

Message

Materials Needed: A glass of water

Have you ever heard of a worldview? Every person has a
worldview. A worldview is the way you see the world
around you. Everyone's worldview is different because
everyone sees the world differently. (*Hold up a clear glass
with water in it.*) For example, look at this glass. If I asked
you what you see, I could get different responses. Someone might say, "I see water." Another person might say, "I
see a glass half full." And then another person might say,

"I see a clean glass." Even though these are all different answers, they are correct. We just see things differently.

However, God wants us to see the world the way He does. We learn about how God see the world through the Bible. This is called a biblical worldview. A biblical worldview is learning the Bible and then making choices that please God based on what the Bible tells us to do. But there is an additional worldview for Christians. It is called a missional worldview. A missional worldview teaches us how God wants us to share what we learn in the Bible with people around the world. The more we learn and do missions, the more we want to share Jesus' love with people all around the world. Let's pray.

Prayer: God, help us to make the Bible and missions a part of every day.

Application Activity: Worldview Test

Challenge: You will have to make many choices this week. Before you make a decision, think if this is something God would want you to do.

Read the following scenarios to the children and have them say which option would be a biblical worldview.

1. Rob really wants to ride his brother Shane's brand-new bicycle, but Shane asks him not to because the bicycle is really too big for Rob and he could get hurt. Rob could sneak behind his brother's back and do it anyway, or Rob could respect his brother's wishes and wait until he grows bigger before he rides it.

2. Amy finds out that her friend Jane is saying some mean things about her at school. Amy could ignore her friend and say bad things about her, or Amy could go to her friend and forgive her.

3. Micah breaks a toy that he had borrowed from a friend. Micah could tell the friend that he lost it or he could admit that he broke it.

Now, discuss how important it is to make choices that reflect what God teaches in the Bible. Also, discuss how part of having a missional worldview is helping others to develop a biblical worldview.

Family Moment

Discuss with the children some of the important biblical and missional views you have that you want to pass on to them. Also, talk about the importance of making decisions based on the Bible.

39. Acts 1:8

Scripture Verse: Acts 1:8

Verse to Memorize: Acts 1:8

Missional Lesson: Children will learn what Acts 1:8 means to them.

Message

Materials Needed: A globe and a Bible

(Hand the globe to one of the children.) Who can tell me what *(child's name)* is holding in her hands? Yes, this is a globe of the earth. In the Scriptures, we find many places where Jesus talks about the earth. Just before Jesus went to heaven, this is what He told the people. *(Read Acts 1:8.)*

(Set the Bible aside, pick up the globe, and point out the places as you explain the following.) Let me show you the areas that Jesus was talking about. Jerusalem is a city located near the Mediterranean Sea in the country of

Israel. Judea is this area around and below Jerusalem. Samaria is the area above Jerusalem. And the uttermost parts of the earth refer to rest of the world. Now let's take this Scripture verse and apply it to us.

(Turn the globe around and point out where you live.) This is our Jerusalem. Jesus wants us to tell our friends and family about Him. This is where missions begins for us. *(Point to the area around your town to include your county and state.)* This area would be our Judea. This is the area where you live, but it represents people that you meet outside of your friends and family. *(Point to the states that surround your area and throughout the rest of North America.)* This area is our Samaria. These are people outside our community. We may or may not know these people, but we can still pray for them, minister to them through missions projects, or go on a missions trip to tell them about Jesus. The last thing Jesus told the disciples was go to the uttermost parts of the earth.

Who can tell me where our uttermost parts of the earth are? Our uttermost parts of the earth are the rest of the world. Jesus wants us to tell every boy, girl, man, and woman of every nation and tribe on the earth about Him.

Jesus wants us to go into *(your city, your state, your nation)* and the world. Wow, now that is quite a lot of people who need to know Jesus. Let's pray and ask God to show us how to get started.

Prayer: God, You said in Acts 1:8 that You will help us to tell others about You. Help us to minister to others like Jesus. And give us the words to tell others about Your greatness and Your salvation.

Application Activity: Color Your World with Missions

Materials Needed: A black and white copy of a world map and markers or crayons
Challenge: Put your map on the wall in your room. Each night before you go to bed think of ways that you can support missions in each of these areas and write them on your map. Pray for missions.

Give each child a copy of a world map. Give each child four different colored crayons. Have them color in the areas representing their Jerusalem, Judea, Samaria, and the uttermost parts of the earth. Encourage them to brainstorm ways that they could support missions in each area. Talk about the different ministries in each area that your church or denomination supports.

Family Moment

Share with your children some of the ministry needs in your community, region, state, country, and world. Discuss how the needs are great, but that many people working together under God's leadership can do amazing things.

40. Missions Education for Children

Scripture Verse: Psalm 78:1–7

Verse to Memorize: Psalm 78:4

Missional Lesson: Children will learn about missions education.

Message

Materials Needed: A globe and a Bible

(*Hold up a globe. As you mention a country, point to the country on the globe.*) Come explore the world with me through missions education. We will take a grand adventure through the Amazon jungles of Brazil, then sail to China where we will board a train for India. Once in India we will hike across the deserts. Grab a jacket. You will need it as we travel through Kazakhstan onto Moscow and then through Europe. Wait a minute. I'm getting a little carried away in my travels. There is a purpose to all these places. In missions education, we learn about all these places to be reminded of what God is doing throughout the world.

We learn about the people in these areas and how they live so that we can pray for them. And also it helps us to know how to pray for the missionaries. When we know about the places and hear the stories from the missionaries we can pray for them more specifically.

But missions education is more than just missionaries' stories, it is about each of us and how God wants us to do missions. God wants us to help pray for and support missionaries, but He also wants us to do missions where we live. It is hard to learn about missions without being motivated to want to do something about missions. In missions education, you learn about the needs around you and how you can do ministry to help people and tell them about Jesus. You also learn Scripture passages and how to apply them to your life.

Wow, there is a lot to missions education! But more than that, it is following Jesus and obeying Him. Let's pray.

Prayer: God, thank You for missions education. Help us to support missions and do missions for You.

Application Activity: Internet Resources

Materials Needed: Internet access and a printer

Go to www.gapassport.com and www.wmucia.com and use the missions information and activities to teach children about missions (activities change monthly).

Family Moment

Explore the missions resources at www.wmustore.com. As a family, discuss the importance of missions learning, praying, giving, and doing. Consider ordering resources to teach ongoing missions education in the home.

41. Caleb Project

Scripture Passage: Psalm 22:7

Verse to Memorize: Psalm 22:7

Missional Lesson: Children will learn what the term *unreached people group* means and what missions agencies are doing to reach these people.

Message

Materials Needed: A map highlighting the 10/40 Window

Have you every heard the term *unreached people group?* This refers to people who have not heard about Jesus. There are groups of people all over the world who have not heard about Jesus. Also, you may have heard of the 10/40 Window. (*Show a map with the area highlighted.*) In this area of the world, there are very few Christians.

At the same time, there are missionaries and missions group around the world who are going to these places to better understand these people and their way of life. One such organization is the Caleb Project. This organization wants to help churches become involved in reaching the remaining unreached peoples of the world. This organization goes into unreached people groups and builds relationships with the people groups.

Basically, researchers go and develop friendships among the people group and record their experiences and interactions with the people. This information is compiled. Then they make the information available to inspire others to support and do missions. These resources are very helpful in helping these churches plan ministry to unreached people groups. Let's pray.

Prayer: God, be with the people learning about unreached people groups. Help them to find information that will help missionaries tell those people about Jesus.

Application Activity: Research Expedition

Materials Needed: Information on people groups
Challenge: Take time to get to know someone from a different country and find more about him or her.

Give children information about two or three different people groups. Divide them into groups and have them create a poster about the people group they learned about. Have them share their research. Go to www.imb.org for information on people groups.

Family Moment

Discuss how important it is for us to respect others' cultures and even their beliefs. Ask your children to share some of the different religious beliefs of others. Help them understand what the Bible says about Jesus being the way to God.

42. The Golden Rule

Scripture Passages: Matthew 7:12; Romans 12:10

Verse to Memorize: Matthew 7:12

Missional Lesson: Children will learn that God wants them to care about others.

Message

I need your help answering a couple of questions. Please, answer yes or no out loud after each question. Does God want us to care about others? Does God want you to treat people as you would want people to treat you?

The Bible says that we should treat others as we want to be treated. Jesus says in Matthew 7:12, "'In everything, do to others what you would want them to do to you.'" In Romans, Paul writes the church in Rome telling them to be devoted to one another in brotherly love and to honor one another above themselves. These verses mean that we should be good to others and even put them before ourselves.

Jesus wants us to treat others well and to care for people every day. For example, God wants us to care for the kid in class that always gets in trouble. He wants us to care for the kid that says bad things and the kid that doesn't dress like everyone else. He wants us to care for the new kid that doesn't fit in and the kid that has a family from a different religion. When we care for people, it shows them that we love them. Through our caring we teach them the love of Jesus. When you treat others well, they will see that there is something different about you and will want to know the reason you are different. You can share with them that you are different because of Jesus. Let's pray.

Prayer: God, help us to see the people around us and to be kind to them. Show us ways to help them, and how to tell them about Jesus.

Application Activity: Helping Others Through Difficult Times

Materials Needed: A piece of poster board to record brainstorming
Challenge: This week, become a new friend to someone at school.

Ask the children to brainstorm situations where they were treated badly or were going through a difficult time. Ask them to share what it was like to experience the situations. Ask them to think about what others did and what others could have done to help them.

Now ask the children to brainstorm a situation where other children were treated badly or went through a difficult time. Then lead the children in discussing how we can care for others as Jesus would. Tell children that, first, we must become aware of those people around us. Second, let them know that we are their friends. Third, show them Jesus.

Family Moment

Have family members discuss how they can care for and minister to those in the community who have been neglected.

IV.

Ministry

43. Ministries to Prisoners' Families

Scripture Verse: Hebrews 13:3

Verse to Memorize: Hebrews 13:3

Missional Lesson: Children will learn about how the Angel Tree ministry helps children.

Message

We hear about crime every night on the news. With every crime peoples' lives are affected. In an instant, lives are changed. When a parent commits a crime and goes to prison, their children are affected. In many cases, children are forced to live with relatives or in foster care. So instantly, they have to get used to a new home. Then the children live with the embarrassment and shame of having a parent in prison and having other children look at them as if there is something wrong with them. No matter how embarrassed the children are, they still miss their parent and struggle with loving him or her; yet they are angry at their parent for what he or she did. Children go through a lot when a parent is put in prison.

There is a Christian organization called Angel Tree that ministers to children whose parents are in prison. Angel Tree helps provide Christmas gifts for these children. In some states they also provide Christian summer camps. Through this ministry, children hear about the love of God and feel the care and love through the volunteers. Camp is a special time when the children get to be around other children who are dealing with the same kind of situation. They can talk with other kids about their parents without being embarrassed or judged. They also have Christian counselors to talk to.

You can help children whose parents are in prison by being a friend to them and by helping other children understand. Let's pray.

Prayer: God, thank You for ministries like Angel Tree that help children in difficult situations to know Your love.

Application Activity: Encouragement Cards

Materials Needed: Paper, markers or crayons, glue, and decorations for cards
Challenge: This week when you hear about someone being put in jail, remember to pray for the children of that person.

Make encouragement cards for children of prisoners. Work through a local prison chaplain to distribute cards. Consider inviting a prison chaplain to come and speak to the children about his or her work.

Family Moment

Look through the newspaper and cut out a couple of crime stories. Discuss the consequences of breaking the law and the hardships it brings to children who are involved. Pray for the criminal, that he or she will find God and repent. Pray for the children and other family members whose lives have been changed, that they will look to God for strength and help. Pray that children will not fall into a life of crime like their parent.

44. Ministering to Persons Affected by Disasters

Scripture Passage: Psalm 40:1–2

Verses to Memorize: Psalm 40:1–2

Missional Lesson: Children will learn about the ministry of disaster relief.

Message

We have all heard about different natural disasters that happen all around the world. In America, we hear about tornadoes, hurricanes, floods, earthquakes, and occasional blizzards in some parts of the country. The water and winds from these natural disasters cause damage to people's homes. They often lose most of their belongings, including food and clothing. They may not have electricity and water, so they are unable to cook. Their houses might be completely destroyed. In most cases there is debris like trees lying all around the yard. During the first couple of months after a natural disaster, people need lots of help.

When disasters happen, missions organizations call on thousands of volunteers from across the nation to go and help those families in need. Some volunteers provide a safe place for children while their parents are receiving help or collecting their belongings. Other volunteers clear trees and other debris from yards and streets. Other volunteers provide meals. Some volunteers distribute clean water, canned foods, and clothing. Other volunteers set up portable trailers for people to take showers. All the volunteers are there to show these hurting people the love of Jesus. Let's close in prayer.

Prayer: God, I pray for the people whose lives are affected by natural disasters. I pray that they see the hope of Jesus in the volunteers that help them.

Application Activity: Safety Drills

Materials Needed: Recruit community service personnel to share with the children
Challenge: This week when you hear about disasters occurring around the world, stop and pray.

Teach children what to do during a natural disaster such as a tornado, a hurricane, or a flood. Consider having a fireman or a police officer come and give a five-minute presentation to children on what to do during a natural disaster (or other disasters that happen in your area).

Ask volunteers to tell the children some things they can do for those in their area when these disasters occur. Have children pray for areas that have just experienced a natural disaster.

Family Moment

Develop a family safety plan for your home and practice the drill as a family. Also, consider giving financially to support a ministry that helps with natural disasters (see resources on p. 177).

45. Ministering to Children Without Homes

Scripture Verse: James 1:27

Verse to Memorize: Matthew 9:37

Missional Lesson: Children will learn that Jesus told His disciples that they are to take care of orphans.

Message

Paul writes in the Book of James that the church is to take care of children without parents. *(Read James 1:27.)*

All around the world there are children who do not have parents. Some have lost their parents in war or to sickness. For others their mother has abandoned them because she cannot take care of them. There are many reasons that children do not have parents. (*If your church is affiliated with an organization that helps care for orphans, share about that ministry and the families that it has created. Show pictures if appropriate.*)

Today there are many ministries around the world to help children without parents find a home. Many churches and organizations support group homes for children. Children may live with 6 to 10 other children in a home with one set of parents. The parents take care of the children as if they were their own. Other churches provide orphanages. At an orphanage there might be 30 or more children who live together with adults who take care of them. There are some groups that help find parents to adopt children. Adoptive parents become the child's real parents and treat them just like they were their parents from birth.

Pray that every child around the world will have parents who love them. Let's pray.

Prayer: Dear God, I pray for all the children of the world, that they might know the love of a parent.

Application Activity: Banner for Children

Materials Needed: A large piece of paper for each child and markers or crayons
Challenge: This week pray daily for orphans to know the love of Jesus and to find a place to call home.

Before the activity, check your local phone book for a children's home in your area. Contact the children's home and ask about sending things to the children living there. During the activity, have each child make a banner for a child in a local children's home. Let the banner read *You are loved.* Let each child decorate his or her banner with pictures and Scripture verses. Have the children sign their first name to every banner. During the week, deliver the banners to the children's home you have contacted.

Pray for the children who will receive these banners and that the children may know the love of God.

Family Moment

Talk with your children about what adoption means. Tell them that parents of adopted children love their adopted children just like you love them. Consider volunteering with your local foster care association to care for children waiting for placement.

46. Ministering to Widows

Scripture Verse: James 1:27

Verse to Memorize: James 1:27

Missional Lesson: Children will learn that God wants Christians to take care of widows.

Message

How many of you have a grandmother, but do not have a grandfather? If your grandfather is deceased, and your grandmother is alive, your grandmother is called a widow. A widow is a woman whose husband has died. God tells the church that it is supposed to take care of widows and make sure that they have the resources they need. (*Consider having a widow share her story.*)

One thing that children can do for widows is to give them a smile and a hug when they see them. I want all the widows who need a little encouragement today to stand up or raise your hand so the children can see you. (*Be sensitive to the widows in your church. If they would be uncomfortable standing, omit it. However, this can be a very beautiful moment in the life of your church.*) Children, I want you to look at all the women standing up or raising their hands and smile and blow kisses at them to show them how much we love them. Now I want the people around them to give them a hug of encouragement and tell them that they are special to them and to God.

Encouraging widows with hugs and smiles is very important. However, children can do more. Children can volunteer to help with yard work. Your family can minister to widows by inviting them to dinner, by providing transportation to the doctor or for shopping, by involving them in family events, by visiting with them weekly, and by phoning them. Let's pray.

Prayer: God, help us to be a source of encouragement to widows in our church and community.

Application Activity: Ministry Project to Widows

Materials Needed: Paper, markers or crayons, glue, and decorations for cards

Challenge: This week call two widows and tell them a funny story.

Make encouragement cards for widows. Decorate and send cards of encouragement to widows in your church and community.

Family Moment

Plan to do a ministry project for a widow in your neighborhood.

47. Ministering to the Poor Through Missions Centers

Scripture Verse: Proverbs 31:9

Verse to Memorize: Proverbs 31:9

Missional Lesson: Children will learn how missions centers help children and their families.

Message

Materials Needed: Place a can of food, a pair of socks, a toothbrush, a cookbook, a Bible, a computer mouse, a reading book, a basketball, and a power bill in a bag.

Hello, boys and girls. I brought some items I want to share with you. As I take each item out of the bag, I want you to tell me what you see. (*Take the items out of the bag and show them to the children.*) All of these are items you might find at a missions center. These centers help meet the basic needs of children and families who live in poverty. However, as they help people obtain needed resources, they also share the love of Jesus with them.

Most missions centers provide food, clothing, and personal items for people who come to them seeking help. Let's look at the other items in our bag. Here is a cookbook. At some missions centers, people are taught how to cook healthy meals for their children. Here is a reading book. At some missions centers, adults and children are taught how to read. Here is a computer mouse. At some missions centers children are taught how to use computers and adults are taught job skills. Here is a basketball. At some missions centers, afterschool activities are provided for children. Here is a bill. Some missions centers are able to help people pay a bill so their electricity will not be turned off. Here is a Bible. At all missions centers, the love of Christ is shared with children and families through caring for the people and providing them with resources to help them to provide for their family.

How can we help missions centers? We can pray for the volunteers and people in need. We can give our good clothes when we outgrow them. We can donate food; we can give toys; we can volunteer to help sort and organize donations; and we can give money to help missions centers stay open. Let's pray and ask God to lead us in how we can help missions centers.

Prayer: God, thank You for providing missions centers that help people in poverty. God, show us what You would have us to do to support missions centers.

Application Activity: A Sweet Treat of Encouragement

Materials Needed: Paper, scissors, markers or crayons, glue, and chocolate bars (mini or regular size)
Challenge: This week clean out your clothes closet and give the clothes that are in good condition to a missions center in your area.

Before the activity, contact a missions center in your town or state and find out how they minister to people. Learn how the children can help the center. During activity time, take about five minutes to share with the children about the specific missions center. Have the children brainstorm ways they might be able to help the missions center. Before the activity, cut white paper to fit around candy bars to make a wrapper. Have children decorate the wrappers with pictures and encouraging words and/or Scripture verses. Wrap the new wrappers around the original wrapper of the candy bar. Take the candy bars to the center to be given out to children or families.

Family Moment

Discuss how missions centers help families similar to yours have the resources they need to live. Plan to visit a missions center and do some volunteer work as a family.

48. Ministering to Women and Children Living in Poverty

Scripture Passage: Matthew 25:42–45

Verse to Memorize: Matthew 25:45

Missional Message: Children will learn about two ministries that minister to families, particularly to women and their children, who live in poverty situations.

Message

Materials Needed: A nice woman's suit jacket, a Bible, and a craft item made in another country

There are many ministries around the world to help people living in poverty. The majority of people living in poverty are women and children. One organization, Woman's Missionary Union® (WMU®), is providing ministries to help women in poverty obtain jobs to support their families. One of these ministries is Christian Women's Job Corps® (CWJC℠). This ministry provides women in need with Christian mentors who will teach them the Bible (*hold up the Bible*) while teaching them skills to help them get a job. CWJC teaches women job skills, provides them with nice work clothes (*hold up the women's business jacket*), and helps them be better parents through parenting and nutrition classes. But the most important role of CWJC is Christian women teaching other women about their spiritual need for Jesus.

Another ministry of WMU is WorldCrafts℠. This ministry provides income for people living in poverty in other countries. WorldCrafts works through missionaries to sell crafts goods from groups overseas. (*Show the children an example of a craft item made in a different country.*) The native crafts are bought through WMU and sold in the United States. This ministry not only provides income for women in poverty, it also provides these families the opportunity to learn about Jesus and for new church to be started.

Let's pray and thank God for these types of ministries that help women break the cycle of poverty.

Prayer: God, thank You for these and other ministries that churches are doing to minister to women and children living in poverty.

Application Activity: Matthew 25:42 Matching Game

Materials Needed: A dozen 5-by-7 cards
Challenge: Go to www.WorldCraftsVillage.com and read the stories of the families that this ministry is helping. Pray for each people group.

Play a matching game with the children based on Matthew 25:42. Make 5-by-7 cards with one of the following words on each card:
Hungry
Give food

Thirsty
Give a drink

Stranger
Welcome and make comfortable

Clothes
Provide clothing

Sick
Provide care to get well

In prison
Visit

Mix up the cards and have the children take turns matching the cards. Have the children discuss these situations and how people can help others in each circumstance. Discuss with the children that when we do something for others, it is like doing it for Jesus.

Tell women and children about ministries that your church supports or go to www.wmu.com/getinvolved/ministry/ to learn more about CWJC and WorldCrafts.

Family Moment

Discuss some of the reasons women and children live in poverty. Parents, share your personal work experiences with your children. Explain that it is a blessing to be able to provide for the basic needs of the family. As a family, discuss how you may be able to get involved with ministries like CWJC and WorldCrafts.

49. Ministering to Children in Hospitals

Scripture Verse: John 15:13

Verse to Memorize: John 15:13

Missional Message: Children will learn about sharing
    Christ with children in hospitals.

Message

Raise your hand if you have ever heard of a doctor being a
missionary. Today, I'm going to tell you about a missionary doctor who lived in a country called Yemen. Yemen is
a very small country next to Saudi Arabia. It is a Muslim
country, so there are very few Christians living in Yemen.
Some Christians wanted to tell the Yemeni people about

Jesus, so they began praying for a way to get into Yemen. Through their prayers they were able to build a hospital for the people in Yemen. One of the Christian doctors that worked in the hospital was Martha Myers.

Martha Myers grew up near Montgomery Alabama. She became a Christian when she was nine years old and was very active at her church. As a child, she knew that when she grew up she wanted to be a missionary. She did not know where she wanted to go, but she knew that was what God wanted her to be. As Martha grew up, she began to prepare herself to be a missionary. She also decided she wanted to be a doctor, so she went to school to learn how to be a doctor.

In medical school she went on a short-term missions trip to work at the hospital in Yemen. After seeing the suffering of the women and children, Martha knew God wanted her there. She returned to the States and completed medical school and seminary training. Then she returned to Yemen.

In Yemen, Dr. Martha cared for women and children by providing much needed health care. She traveled to the villages providing immunizations and basic medical supplies. She gave all that she had to heal the hurts of the people of Yemen. She shared the love of God through her love and care for the people until her death. Let us pray for the people of Yemen who still come to the hospital for physical healing, and hear about Jesus through doctors like Dr. Martha.

Prayer: God, we pray for the people in Yemen, that they may know Your grace, love, and peace through Jesus.

Application Activity: Activity Bag Book for Hospitalized Children

Materials Needed: Crayons, coloring book pages, white paper, stickers, construction paper, sticks of gum, colored paper, resealable plastic bags, stapler

Challenge: This week think about children who spend a lot of time in the hospital. Think of ways that you can show them the love of Jesus, then do one of the actions.

Teach children that they can show love to sick children, like Dr. Martha, in their area by providing an activity bag. Prepare supplies so that each child may make at least one activity bag book.

Follow these directions:

Page 1—Place two or three crayons and a sheet from a coloring book in a bag.

Page 2—Place a plain half sheet of paper and several loose stickers in a bag.

Page 3—On a half-sheet of construction paper, print the words of a Bible verse such as "God is love" (1 John 4:8). Cut the paper into six jigsaw puzzle pieces. Put the pieces in a bag.

Page 4—Put two sticks of gum in a bag. Print a message on plain paper to add to the bag. Use a message such as *Jesus loves you, God hears all prayers,* or *God made you.*

Direct each child to print on a colorful paper a title such as *A Book for You* or *My Fun Book.* Allow children to slide the cover sheets into resealable plastic bags. Stack the bag pages with the openings at the top and staple the book together along one side, being careful not to catch any of the contents of the bags in the staples.

Then deliver the books to a hospital that cares for children in your area.

Pray for the children of Yemen, that others will come and care for them.

Family Moment

Research Yemen and then discuss how life for your family would be different if you lived in Yemen. Pray for the Christians in Yemen and in other countries where it is dangerous for them to be known as Christians.

(For more information about Martha Myers, read *The Story of Martha Myers* by Barbara Joiner.)

50. Annie Armstrong/WMU

Scripture Verse: 1 Corinthians 3:9

Verse to Memorize: 1 Corinthians 3:9

Missional Lesson: Children will learn about the life and legacy of Annie Armstrong.

Message

How many have heard the name of Annie Armstrong? Annie Armstrong lived many years ago and inspired women and men to support missions through giving and praying. In her lifetime she wrote thousands of letters encouraging missionaries and challenging Christians to support missions. In 1888, she was able to bring together women from ten states to organize a woman's group called Woman's Missionary Union® (WMU®). Against criticism and opposition, the women organized with the purpose of praying for missions, giving to support missions, and learning about missions work.

Annie pressed forward and developed an organization of women that supported missions. She traveled to encourage women to support missions and start WMU groups. She also spent time ministering to Native American Indians. The Annie Armstrong Easter Offering® for North American Missions was named after Annie in 1934. This offering has supported the work of thousands of missionaries in North America.

Annie's determination created a network of women all over the world with the purpose of supporting and doing missions. Let's pray.

Prayer: God, thank You for Annie Armstrong and for her love and dedication to You.

Application Activity: A Letter Like Annie's

Challenge: Write a report about a missionary you have learned about and share the story with a friend or family member.

Have children write a letter or draw a picture telling someone why giving to missions is important. Discuss how important it is to support missions.

Family Moment

Share with your children the people in your life who have taught and supported you and your family along the way. Share the story of a missionary that you admire.

51. Lottie Moon

Scripture Verse: Acts 20:35

Verse to Memorize: Acts 20:35

Missional Lesson: Children will learn about the life and legacy of Lottie Moon.

Message

Between Thanksgiving and Christmas we often hear the name Lottie Moon. The reason her name is so familiar is because each year around Christmastime Southern Baptist take a missions offering that was named in her honor. So what did she do to have an offering named after her?

The story began in Virginia in 1840. She grew up wealthy and very well educated. Days after her 18th birthday Lottie became a Christian. She also felt called to missions. She was appointed as a missionary to China on July 7, 1873.

Lottie began work in Tengchow and then moved inland where she was the only foreigner. Lottie won the hearts of the people. Her witness and teaching methods led to the establishment of a network of churches. As she was ministering to people in China, she was also diligent about writing back home to encourage others to come to China. It was such a letter that led Annie Armstrong to call women to support Lottie. The first offering the women collected was enough to send three women to China.

Lottie Moon served in China 39 years. Towards the end of her life, China was hit with flood, famine, and war. Lottie gave all that she had to the people, including her food. A ship came to take Lottie back home to be cared for, but it was too late. Lottie died Christmas Eve 1912.

How appropriate that the Lottie Moon Christmas Offering® was officially named in her honor in 1918. Lottie dedicated her life to ministering to others and encouraging Christians to support missions. Let's pray.

Prayer: God, thank You for the example that Lottie Moon is to us today. And thank You for all the people that the Lottie Moon Christmas Offering® has brought to Jesus.

Application Activity: A Different Place

Challenge: This week eat with chopsticks for five or more meals. After each meal, pray for the people in China.

If possible, set up a section of the room without any tables or chairs. Have the children take off their shoes and sit in a circle. Give each child a pair of chopsticks and have them try to pick up small items with their chopsticks. Discuss if it would be hard or easy to use chopsticks for every meal. Discuss how Lottie made the choice to fit into the culture by dressing and living like the Chinese. Discuss how missionaries today follow her example.

Family Moment

This week plan a dinner with Chinese food using chopsticks while sitting around the coffee table eating. Also, consider having the family take off their shoes at the door for one week.

52. You Can Be On Mission with God

Scripture Verse: Matthew 5:16

Verse to Memorize: Matthew 5:16

Missional Lesson: Children will learn how they can be
on mission with God.

Message

God is at work in the world and He wants to use you to
accomplish His work of telling others about Jesus. OK, OK,
you may be thinking, "I'm just a kid. How can I help
God?" Well, first God desires to have a relationship with
us. We develop a relationship with Him when we become

a Christian and then seek to know more about Him through prayer and Bible study. After we spend time getting to know God, He shows us what He is doing and invites us to join Him in His work. OK, is that so hard? God wants to know us and then He wants us to work for Him. The hard part is next. God tells us what He wants us to do. The things that God asks us to do are hard because they are not the same priorities as those of the world we live in. When we choose to follow Him, we may have to make some changes in our life. Then we need to trust and obey God.

The struggle to follow God is a little like learning how to ride a bicycle without training wheels. You have seen other kids riding bicycles and you really want to be able to ride by yourself. However, you are afraid because you could fall, or you really are not sure if you can do it without training wheels or an adult holding you up. You just have to believe and pedal. Once you start pedaling, you adjust your body to keep your balance. Before you know it, you are riding your bicycle. The difference with being on mission with God is that God is in control. You were in control of the bicycle and it was the belief in yourself that helped you pedal without help. However, when you decide to be on mission with God, you put your faith, trust, and life into His hands. He will use you to tell others about Jesus.

You still may be thinking, "I'm just a kid. How can I help?" Remember, God has already prepared you or will prepare you for what He asks you to do. God does not have limits for who can be on mission with Him. He may be preparing you to be a missionary 15 years from now or He may be preparing you to tell a parent or friend about His love. I pray each of you will choose to be on mission with God. Let's close in prayer.

Prayer: God, thank You for allowing us the privilege to be on mission with You.

Application Activity: Fill in the Blank

Challenge: Make a yearlong commitment to seek God and follow wherever He leads.

God, I'm happy when _____.
It is hard to trust God when _____.
It is hard for me to understand _____.
If I could ask you a question it would be _____.

God, I want to be a _____ when I grow up.

Lead each child to fill in the blanks and share their thoughts. Tell them that God has a wonderful plan, and that wherever they are in life, God wants them to join Him on mission.

Family Moment

Discuss what it means to be on mission with God. Discuss ways that your family can be on mission with God.

V.

Family Debriefing

Family
Debriefing

1. Has *Missions Moments* helped you look at missions differently? If so, explain and share with your family.

   _____
   _____
   _____
   _____
   _____

2. As a family, discuss some things you have learned through doing activities in *Missions Moments* that stand out in your mind.

   _____
   _____
   _____
   _____
   _____

3. What have you learned that you want to personally apply to your life?

_____

_____

_____

_____

_____

4. What have you learned that you would like your family to apply to their lives?

_____

_____

_____

_____

_____

5. Take a moment and write one or two specific things that your family will seek to do to live a missions lifestyle.

_____

_____

_____

_____

_____

6. Plan several ministry projects for your family to participate in this year.

_____

_____

_____

_____

_____

VI.

Resources

Resources

For an extended listing of missions agencies, an excellent resource is *Mission Handbook: U.S. and Canadian Protestant Ministries Overseas,* edited by Dotsey Welliver and Minnette Northcutt and published by EMIS (Evangelism and Missions Information Service), a division of the Billy Graham Center. For ordering information, call (630) 752-7158; or visit www.billygrahamcenter.org.

Web sites
Angel Tree: www.pfm.org
Caleb Project: www.calebproject.org
Children in Action: www.wmucia.com
Christian Women's Job Corps: www.wmu.com/getinvolved/ministry/cwjc/
Chronological Bible Storying: www.chronologicalbiblestorying.com
Volunteer Connection: www.wmu.com/getinvolved/ministry/volunteer/
Girls in Action: www.gapassport.com
Royal Ambassadors: www.kidzplace.org/adult/royalambassadors/ra.asp

International Mission Board (IMB): www.imb.org
North American Mission Board (NAMB): www.namb.net
WMU (Woman's Missionary Union): www.wmu.com
WorldCrafts: www.WorldCraftsVillage.com
Wycliffe Bible Translators: www.wycliffe.org

Books
The Story of Lottie Moon by Cathy Butler
The Story of Annie Armstrong by Cathy Butler
The Story of Martha Myers by Barbara Joiner
The Story of WMU by Jeanie McLean

Scripture Index

Topical Index

Thank you!

Your purchase of this book and other WMU products supports the mission and ministries of WMU. To find more great resources, visit our online store at www.wmustore.com or talk with one of our friendly customer service representatives at 1-800-968-7301.

For more information about children's missions education, visit www.wmu.com/orgs/children.

***WMU*®**
Discover the Joy of Missions SM
www.wmu.com

New GA Song ♪

Change the World:
Mission Songs for
Children
W047103, $14.99

Get ready to be blown away!
**This contemporary and dynamic CD is incredible.
It features worship and camp songs, two versions
of "We've a Story to Tell," and a brand-new GA
song. You and your girls will love it! A helpful
songbook is also included.**

Listen to *Change the World* in your GA meetings,
home, or car. Kids of all ages will enjoy listening,
learning, and singing these great mission songs.